Advent is a time in whi ░░░░░░
we practice, knowing ░░░░░ MW00774684
in the waiting. In this way, *Advent is the Story* is a gift to the ░░░
Bringing these readings alongside our prayers of longing and our
lighting of candles will help us to reorient our own stories around the
Truest Story—one in which the promises extend well before our own
beginnings and keep us until the end.

ELIZABETH HARWELL, founder of Liturgy Wood

This is an advent book that goes where many others do not. Rather
than focusing solely on the events directly surrounding the birth of
Jesus, Spanjer casts a wider net, placing the beauty of the Christmas
story firmly within the context of the epic tale of creation, order,
disorder, redemption and restoration. From Eden to Babel, from the
promised land to the New Jerusalem, this book reminds us that all
of history has been marked by the same drumbeat of hope, as God
relentlessly pursues the people he loves, stopping at nothing to make
his dwelling place among them.

HEIDI JOHNSTON, author of *Life in the Big Story: Your Place in God's Unfolding Plan*

In *Advent is the Story,* the authors help the reader see that the birth
of the Messiah was the culmination of the promises, prophecies,
and religious practices observed by Israel. Redemptive history is
filled with God working through people who exhibited faith and
failure, hope and despair, all the time pointing toward the one who
would make all things right. The temple was not just a building,
the ceremonies were not just arbitrary movements, and the sacrifices were not meaningless slaughter. Everything points toward
Jesus who would come at just the right time, to fulfill all that came

before, through his birth, life, death and resurrection. *Advent is the Story* reminds us that God has directed the lives of His people from Adam until today and He will continue to do so until He returns as the glorious King.

A.D. BAUER, author of *How To See: Reading God's Word with New Eyes*

Weaving together scriptural, theological, and literary insights, Daniel Spanjer has crafted a wonderful Advent devotional, fitting for any Christian. More than this, in a small space, he has provided a simple, yet not simplistic, presentation of the breadth and depth of Christian theology and biblical study that even those unfamiliar with the Faith would find compelling and informative.

TIMOTHY D PADGETT, resident theologian at The Colson Center

Christmas is a time of year at which we as Protestant, Evangelical, and American Christians are a bit more open to see things from a broader perspective. Dan Spanjer has capitalized on this opportunity so that we may delight in a bigger story that is about God and his Kingdom and our citizenship in it. Spanjer presents Advent as an invigorating invitation to become excited about a deeper celebration of Christmas that spills over into the entirety of life.

My family will follow the daily readings this December so that we may catch the joy and anticipation of the holiday while being reminded of the great and true overarching story of which we are a part. I plan to recommend Dan's work to my students as well so that their families will catch the vision.

I'm more excited for Christmas already!

TRIPP ALMON, director of Summit Semester/Summit.org

ADVENT
is the STORY

Merry
Christmas

Dave & Barb

DANIEL R. SPANJER

ADVENT
is the STORY

Seeing the Nativity
throughout Scripture

A COLLECTION
OF READINGS FOR THE
ADVENT SEASON

SQUARE HALO BOOKS

In Christian art, the square halo identified a living person presumed to be a saint. Square Halo Books is devoted to publishing works that present contextually sensitive biblical studies, and practical instruction consistent with the Doctrines of the Reformation. The goal of Square Halo Books is to provide materials useful for encouraging and equipping the saints.

©2022 Square Halo Books, Inc.
P.O. Box 18954
Baltimore, MD 21206
www.SquareHaloBooks.com

The artwork on the cover is a detail from
The Mystical Nativity by Sandro Botticelli.

ISBN 978-1-941106-23-5
Library of Congress Control Number: 2021920355

Printed in the United States of America

For Charles
Sharrod Makenzie
—a man who unabashedly
lived for the coming
of his king.

INTRODUCTION

As a pastor, I have observed two encouraging places of maturity and growth in the evangelical Church over the past two decades: a maturing appreciation for how the Church in history has marked time using a Christ-centered calendar, and a growing commitment to reading the Scriptures as one story with Jesus at the center. *Advent Is the Story* pulls wonderfully in both directions. Dr. Spanjer, my fellow elder, interlocutor, and loyalist in the Kingdom, has brought these two pieces together as a gift to be shared with the Church.

His book, as you've guessed, is for Advent. It is a collection of daily readings and reflections for the season and on through the first week of Christmas. Advent, long considered the beginning of the Church's year, is meant to orient the Church away from all the places her attention has drifted and back to the central story of the world, the coming of Jesus. During Advent, Christians for centuries have paused everything else, seeking to prepare hearts and lives to welcome our Savior, who comes to us. At the heart of Advent is our celebration of God's love at his coming to us in Jesus and our longing for his final coming to put all things right. And this book celebrates that.

But it is far more than a devotional. *Advent Is the Story* leads us back through both the Old and New Testaments to unfold,

one story at a time, how the coming of Jesus has been at the
center of the world all along. From creation in Genesis to new
creation in Revelation, *Advent Is the Story* walks the reader
through the twists and turns of redemptive history to show how
the reign of King Jesus and his generous and gracious Kingdom
come to earth have been the heartbeat of history. Given that
orientation, the reflections here may be different from those in
other Advent devotionals you have encountered. *Advent Is the
Story* is a biblical theology for Advent. In my experience as a
pastor, this is just where the Church has often been thin, starving
for the theological reflection that this book provides. Dr. Spanjer
opens up wide, expansive views of the coming of Jesus, inviting
us out of the shallows of an overly sentimentalized season and
into the depth and richness of the biblical narrative, with fresh
perspectives that deepen our hopes and sharpen our longings for
Jesus and his Kingdom.

A few words about the structure of the book. Six interspersed
topical essays carry us along throughthe flow of the daily
readings. But the essays are separate from the readings and may
be read at any time. They appear in an intentional order: "The
Word," "The Temple," "The King," "The Exodus," "The Sacrifice,"
"The Now and Not Yet." At the center of each daily reading stands
a passage of scripture. Paragraphs that introduce that passage
sketch out the surrounding biblical and theological landscape,
pointing out contours and features of the biblical narrative. So
when we read the passage itself, we benefit from a wise and
reliable guide for where to look and what we will see. After the
scripture for the day, a paragraph or two connect all that has
come before to Jesus, the One who has come and is coming again.

After Christmas, the order is flipped. The Scripture passage is still at the center, but since Jesus has come in the flesh, each daily devotion begins with a contemplation of that reality, followed by the scripture and a theological reflection.

Advent Is the Story means to give us fresh eyes to see that at the very center of the grand story of redemption is Christmas. In Jesus, a loving God took on human flesh to dwell with his people. Through a surprising humility, God restores his relationship with his world. Jesus Christ is now the hope of every human heart, the realization of every human longing for restoration. Humanity has been recreated and perfectly loved by God in Jesus. And so Christmas is not merely a sentiment. It is the reality that makes sense of all human history. And in this way, Advent, with its blessed hope and promise, *is the story.*

   —Luke Le Duc, senior pastor of
     Wheatland Presbyterian Church,
     Lancaster, PA

ADVENT
is the STORY

THE WORD

People in the ancient world did not see a clear distinction between nature and words. Moderns have come to believe that the universe is a purely mechanical engine that operates according to mindless, purposeless natural laws. The ancient Egyptians, Meso-potamians, Canaanites, and Assyrians, however, believed that the cosmos obeyed the decisions of the gods. Thus, everything in the world moved according to the will of beings and so had purpose. Trees, birds, and water followed the dictates of intelligent deities.

While moderns believe that the things of this universe are moved by blind forces, the ancients believed that everything around them was part of a story told by powerful beings. Moses himself grew up seeing the world this way until Yahweh revealed to him a radically different view of the cosmos. In the creation story, God told Moses that the universe is not a language spoken by gods but rather that it has meaning because of the word that he spoke. Contrary to both modern and ancient beliefs, the cosmos operates according to God's word.

In Genesis 1, Moses writes that God created the world. He brought all the elements of this incredible universe into existence out of nothing. From the mind of an omnipotent and awesome creator came stars, light, space, matter, and time. Moses then informs us that while God created the cosmos, it was, on its own, "without form and void." In other words, the universe was meaningless and disordered; it had no purpose or meaning in and of itself, but in verse 2 of Genesis 1 everything changes. The Bible says that the Holy Spirit hovered over a chaotic universe—then God spoke. Through the remainder of Genesis 1, it is the words spoken by God that transform the disordered cosmos into purposeful order. God puts light and darkness, water and land, animals and plants into their proper places; by the word of God the random stuff of the universe became a place of beauty and function. Moses makes it clear that nothing else other than the word of God can give anything meaning or purpose.

After describing the creation of the world, Moses tells the story of human history using the same pattern he laid out in Genesis 1—a pattern defined by the transition from chaos to order. In Genesis 2, God speaks commands to Adam and Eve: be fruitful and multiply, tend the garden, and do not eat of the tree of the knowledge of good and evil. These words from God not only gave humanity purpose and meaning, but by obeying those words Adam and Eve would bring order to the rest of the earth as well. Their obedience to his commandments would have transformed the wild earth into an ordered garden, like the one into which God had graciously placed them.

In Genesis 3 Moses records that rather than obey God's life-giving words, Adam and Eve chose disobedience which not only subjected them to death, but also condemned the entire world to disorder. God had created our first parents to dwell in a place governed by his word, but they chose to believe the serpent's lies and so brought the chaos of thorns, thistles, and death into the world God once called good. The peace they had enjoyed disintegrated into disease and evil as they tore the balance and meaning of the ordered universe into tatters. Despite their disobedience, God did not leave humanity to suffer in a broken world without hope. Into a world, that because of sin, was reverting to the condition of being "formless and void," God spoke again.

Amid his judgment upon the serpent, God spoke a new word that was neither commandment nor mere prediction about the future. God spoke a promise about what he would do to restore both humanity and his creation to a state of order. He promised that one day a Champion would come who would restore order by crushing the one whose word had brought death into the world. God's word in Genesis 3:15 was his final act of the creation narrative for by this word he spoke into reality the future salvation of his people from the corruption of sin.

Since the fall, sin has dragged human beings and their world towards the ultimate meaninglessness of death. In judgment, God turned Adam and Eve over to the final disorder of the grave, which now serves as the destination for all people. But God spoke once again and exerted his power of creation against chaos. God promised to reverse the evil brought upon the universe by humanity's treason. He described this reversal as the development of an enmity between the seed of the woman and the seed of the serpent. This promise meant that one day people would turn away from Satan's lies to follow Yahweh's word once again. One day his word will restore this broken world in anticipation of restoring his people back to himself.

The Scriptures, therefore, are the record of God speaking. Until God called to him, Abraham lived according to words spoken by his family and friends. The Creator's simple command to leave home reoriented Abraham's life. He turned away from the familiar patterns of his world to follow Yahweh. Paul argues in Romans 4 that Abraham became the father of all the faithful through his obedience to God, because Abraham chose to live his entire life by God's word, even though doing so meant he had to leave his own life behind. The Bible calls all of God's people to follow Abraham's example and, by obeying God's word, return order to a disordered world.

The power of God's word is no more evident anywhere than in the story of the Exodus. At the burning bush in Exodus 3, God spoke a new reality to Moses which shattered the world of the Egyptian gods. He called up the plagues and delivered the promise of the pascal lamb to the Hebrews. In an awesome display of his power, he parted the Red Sea for his people, then brought the chaos of that same sea down on the heads of Egypt's mighty army. From Sinai Yahweh spoke the word of his law to establish a new way of life for the Hebrews, a law that set Israel apart from all other nations. By the spoken word, Yahweh directed Moses, called Samuel, chose David, and judged Israel.

God gave his good law to the Hebrews, but such is sin that it corrupts the human heart and entices mankind to strive against its Creator. Although God gave Israel structure and purpose in his plan of redemption, Israel still chose the disorder of idolatry over his laws. Like the judgment he delivered in Genesis 3, God confirmed to Israel disobeying his word brought the same kind of disorder and chaos into the promised land that Adam and Eve had brought into Eden. In the conquests of Israel and Judah, and through the exile, Yahweh's judgment proved as devastating to the Hebrews as the flood waters were to Noah's peers and the crashing waves of the Red Sea were to the Egyptian soldiers. In his judgments of sin, God gives people over to the chaos that they desire more than obedience to his word. Babylon and Assyria shattered Israel's peace with war. Pagan nations dragged Israel's people from a bountiful land governed by God's word into a devastating exile. Israel's judgment was a painful reenactment of the walk Adam and Eve made from the garden to a ground tortured by thorns and thistles.

As Jerusalem and its temple lay in ruins, the Hebrews must have feared that all hope was lost. But God would not allow his people's sin to thwart his glorious plan to redeem his sinful people. Through the prophets, God spoke again and promised to restore what sin had destroyed. He uttered words of promise that would commence a second creation of the world that would begin in the tiny town of Bethlehem, spread to Judea, Samaria and, ultimately, throughout the entire world.

Yahweh's word will ultimately bring order to a world made chaotic by sin in the same way that it brought order to the formlessness of the primeval earth. In, by, and under Jesus Christ, Yahweh promises to establish a final kingdom in which his every word reigns—a kingdom which death and disorder never again destroy.

DECEMBER 1

Judgment and Promise

In Genesis 3, Moses tells the story of humanity's fall from paradise to life in a broken world. In Genesis 1 God created the wonders and beauty of the cosmos out of void and darkness. Genesis 2 describes God's greatest work as he bestowed his image on Adam and Eve and so enters into an intimate relationship with his creation. But the creation of mankind implies more than a static relationship: God created Adam and Eve so that they would imitate Him by governing the earth just as the triune God governs the vast universe. As he brought order to the universe by his word, so he tasked humanity with bringing order, goodness, and beauty to the raw material of the earth by obeying his word. He commanded Adam and Eve to grow Eden's Garden until they would one day bring the entire globe under the generous reign of King Yahweh. By the end of chapter 2, the universe existed in beautiful harmony with its Creator, and the earth brought forth its bounty under the godly governance of its human lords. Moses' description shows a humanity that was whole and good. Man and woman lived together in love and respect. Their nakedness demonstrated that they related to one another happily, without fear or anxiety before God and each other.

But then we come to chapter 3, the story Christians refer to as "the fall." Into a world organized and made beautiful by God's word slithered a crafty serpent. He came to Eve not with threats or violence, but with a lie. He argued that God's word was not bountiful but miserly; God's word, the serpent claimed, kept her from the best fruit, the fruit of the tree of good and evil, and thus from the fullness of God's creation. In other words, the serpent insinuated, the Creator reigned over the garden selfishly so that he might keep Adam and Eve from the best things (Genesis 3:5). The lie encouraged Eve to value the fruit of the tree of the knowledge of good and evil over God's word.

Moses records that Eve "saw that the tree was good for food, and that it was a delight to the eyes." (Genesis 3:6) Eve believed the serpent and so rebelled against the kingdom of Yahweh in order to join a moral order based on a word other than God's. Adam joined Eve so that they might become the ones who distinguish good from evil rather than trust God to do so. But as the first humans savored the taste of that fruit, they realized the terrible truth hidden behind the lie—God's word is the only source of beauty, truth, and goodness. Vulnerability which had been the foundation of their relationship splintered into fear and anxiety.

As the first man and woman plunged further into the horrors precipitated by their treason, God came to the garden to speak with his precious children. In their fear, Adam and Eve admitted to God what he already knew—they had rejected his word and allowed themselves to be seduced by the liar's word. At this point God called Adam, Eve, and the serpent so that he could pronounce judgment on their sinful rejection of his good and wise reign. God had warned them that on the day that they ate of the tree of the knowledge of good and evil they would surely die. This judgment was to be a physical and spiritual execution. It is difficult to imagine the terror building in our first parents' hearts. They had only known eternal bliss and happiness, yet now they faced a dreadful sentence for having rejected their Creator's kingship.

God began with the serpent. Not only had he lied, but he had attempted to subvert God's plan to spread goodness, truth, and beauty across the entire globe through human obedience. Worse, the serpent had declared the holy God to be a liar. For this God judged Satan with the humiliation of scraping through the dust and dirt of the world with no hope of achieving nobility or respect. But God went further when he delivered what must have been a shocking surprise. God declared that Adam and Eve would have children! To have children, Adam and Eve would live; they would not die this day. At the very moment of their judgment, they discovered that their lives would be part of a much larger story. The serpent's seed, all those who declare ultimate loyalty to kings other than the holy God, would grow along side of those who obey God's word. The two peoples would vie with one another until the Enemy's champion finally delivered God's Champion a devastating blow. But God promised that in the end, Eve's seed would finally crush the serpent's head.

Through this violent promise, God revealed his plan to bring his people back into relationship with Himself, to restore the garden, and to end the chaos sin had unleashed on the world. Adam and Eve must have asked themselves, who will this Champion be and when might he come? This question would shape the lives and longings of God's people for the next two thousand years.

GENESIS 3

Now the serpent was craftier than any other beast of the field that the Lord God had made. He said to the woman, "Did God actually say, 'You shall not eat of any tree in the garden'?" And the woman said to the serpent, "We may eat of the fruit of the trees in the garden, but God said, 'You shall not eat of the fruit of the tree that is in the midst of the garden, neither shall you touch it, lest you die.'" But the serpent said to the woman, "You will not surely die. For God knows that when you eat of it your eyes will be opened, and you will be like God, knowing good and evil." So, when the woman saw that the tree was good for food, and that it was a delight to the eyes, and that the tree was to be desired to make one wise, she took of its fruit and ate, and she also gave some to her husband who was with her, and he ate. Then the eyes of both were opened, and they knew that they were naked. And they sewed fig leaves together and made themselves loincloths.

And they heard the sound of the Lord God walking in the garden in the cool of the day, and the man and his wife hid themselves from the presence of the Lord God among the trees of the garden. But the Lord God called to the man and said to him, "Where are you?" And he said, "I heard the sound of you in the garden, and I was afraid, because I was naked, and I hid myself." He said, "Who told you that you were naked? Have you eaten of the tree of which I commanded you not to eat?" The man said, "The woman whom you gave to be with me, she gave me fruit of the tree, and I ate."

Then the Lord God said to the woman, "What is this that you have done?" The woman said, "The serpent deceived me, and I ate." The Lord God said to the serpent,

"Because you have done this, cursed are you above all livestock and above all beasts of the field; on your belly you shall go, and dust you shall eat all the days of your life.

I will put enmity between you and the woman, and between your offspring and her offspring; he shall bruise your head, and you shall bruise his heel."

To the woman he said,

"I will surely multiply your pain in childbearing; in pain you shall bring forth children. Your desire shall be contrary to your husband, but he shall rule over you."

And to Adam he said,

"Because you have listened to the voice of your wife and have eaten of the tree of which I commanded you,

'You shall not eat of it,' cursed is the ground because of you; in pain you shall eat of it all the days of your life; thorns and thistles it shall bring forth for you; and you shall eat the plants of the field. By the sweat of your face you shall eat bread, till you return to the ground, for out of it you were taken; for you are dust, and to dust you shall return."

The man called his wife's name Eve, because she was the mother of all living. And the Lord God made for Adam and for his wife garments of skins and clothed them.

Then the Lord God said, "Behold, the man has become like one of us in knowing good and evil. Now, lest he reach out his hand and take also of the tree of life and eat, and live forever—" therefore the Lord God sent him out from the garden of Eden to work the ground from which he was taken. He drove out the man, and at the east of the garden of Eden he placed the cherubim and a flaming sword that turned every way to guard the way to the tree of life.

Advent is the Story

God demonstrated his justice by judging those who had broken his law. But this judgment also contained a gracious and generous promise of God's provision. First, God delayed the punishment that he had promised Adam and Eve and they did not die the day they ate of the forbidden fruit. Instead, God would bring the complete judgment owed to Adam and Eve on another. Second, Adam and Eve, who could not be trusted to obey God in paradise, would not be the ones to restore humanity back to his good reign. Adam and Eve would have to wait patiently for one of their children to lead them back into a relationship with their God. This champion would be hobbled by a terrible strike on his heel. But the blow would land as the Champion's heel came down on Satan's head.

This text teaches us how to look at the history of mankind since God cast Adam and Eve out of Eden. The history of the world is a story of two peoples: those who follow Satan by declaring ultimate loyalty to any king other than King Yahweh, and those who look, long, and wait for the Champion to restore people to their Creator. For this group, the word of God remains their only hope—the power that alone can orient all of life around the only Good King.

DECEMBER 2

The Promise of Abel

In Genesis 4, Moses begins the history of the fallen world. God's judgment on the serpent established the pattern of life outside of the garden. The serpent would have progeny, a seed, which would grow and expand. But Eve would also have a seed which would multiply. The children of Eve would stand opposed to God's enemies and so begin clearing the way back to friendship with God. No matter how man may tell the story of his past—according to successful and failed nations, power and servitude, humanitarianism and evil—Genesis 3 teaches us to see history as it actually is. All people, nations, institutions, laws, and economies belong to one of two seeds at war with one another. This historic and cosmic struggle will end in a battle not between the peoples but between a single offspring of the woman and a single offspring of Satan. God's champion will destroy Satan's champion and so restore God's perfect rule over the world.

In Genesis 4, Adam and Eve are presented with a very personal

dimension of this story. Adam and Eve had two children, Abel
and Cain. In Genesis 4:4 Moses records that God had regard (in
Hebrew, *yisa*) for Abel's sacrifice which meant that Abel's faithfulness drew him into an intimate relationship with God. Cain, on
the other hand, remained distant from Yahweh. The older brother
was outraged at his younger brother's place of honor before God
and in the family. To Adam and Eve, however, it must have seemed
that God's prophecy in Genesis 3 was being fulfilled before their
eyes. Abel's friendship with God made him an enemy of the
serpent. Perhaps this special relationship with Abel meant that
he was the man of God's promise. By sacrificing the costly fat of
his prized animals, the younger brother showed his willingness to
organize his life around a deep love for God, his true king. Unlike
his brother, Cain, Abel did not reluctantly bring his sacrifices to
God as a matter of routine but joyfully as the priority of his life.
For a shepherd to give the best of his flock meant that he managed
his entire life for one purpose—to bring the firstborn and the fat
portions, the most delicate and delectable parts, to God.

According to Moses, Abel offered sacrifices to God in a way
that was unique compared to the kinds of sacrifices that people
offered during the time that he was writing Genesis. Those who
lived in the Ancient Near East would have been put off by Moses'
description of Abel's work. Nearly all peoples of that period relied
on priests to bring food to their gods twice a day, wait for the gods
to visit the food, and then bring what remained to the king or the
head of the household. People saw sacrifices as their responsibility
to feed their gods, for they believed that they were the farmers for
the gods. But Abel's sacrifice was nothing like the ritual behaviors
of Moses' time. Abel brought sacrifices out of his best, not to feed
God, but rather to honor and love him. Although God's people

would not have had a clear idea about God's view of sacrifices until he gave the law to Moses, Abel's pleasing sacrifice taught the seed of the woman to fellowship with God through gifts of worship. Setting aside the firstborn of the flock not only proved that the worshiper recognized God as king but also demonstrated that relationship with God was the most essential thing in life. By killing the sacrifice, God's people also affirmed that a chasm existed between themselves and God which resulted from their own sin. Sacrifices reminded them that fellowship, communion, and favor with God could be restored only through death.

Abel ordered his life by a love for God which must have convinced Adam and Eve that God was realizing his promise of redemption in him. And yet by Genesis 4:5, Moses reveals that sin was far deadlier than they could have imagined. Abel's older brother harbored a dangerous jealousy in his heart, for Cain chose to blame his brother for his strained relationship with God rather than his disobedience. Cain could not see that keeping the fruit of his labor for himself, rather than committing it to Yahweh, drew his heart away from love of Yahweh to a deadly idolatry.

God gave Cain a warning which should have driven him to repentance and humility, but instead drove him to jealousy. Cain devised a plan to remove Abel so that he could assume the position of favored son. He jealously desired define good and evil himself and so eat the same fruit that his parents had tasted. In rebellion to God Cain struck his brother down. In Cain it became clear that the seed of the serpent would choose self over a right relationship with Yahweh. To his mother and father, Abel's death proved that he was not the seed of promise.

God's prophecy in Genesis 3 said that the seed of the woman would strike the seed of the serpent on the head, but in this story

Cain crushed Abel's head. It seemed that not only had the seed of the serpent won, but also that God had failed. After a painful silence following Abel's death, God gave Eve another son, who would carry on her seed according to God's great promise to bring his people back to himself.

GENESIS 4

Now Adam knew Eve his wife, and she conceived and bore Cain, saying, "I have gotten a man with the help of the Lord." And again, she bore his brother Abel. Now Abel was a keeper of sheep, and Cain a worker of the ground. In the course of time Cain brought to the Lord an offering of the fruit of the ground, and Abel also brought of the firstborn of his flock and of their fat portions. And the Lord had regard for Abel and his offering, but for Cain and his offering he had no regard. So Cain was very angry, and his face fell. The Lord said to Cain, "Why are you angry? Why has your face fallen? If you do well, will you not be accepted? And if you do not do well, sin is crouching at the door. Its desire is contrary to you, but you must rule over it."

Cain spoke to Abel his brother. And when they were in the field, Cain revolted against his brother Abel and killed him. Then the Lord said to Cain, "Where is Abel your brother?" He said, "I do not know; am I my brother's keeper?" And the Lord said, "What have you done? The voice of your brother's blood is crying to me from the ground. And now you are cursed from the ground, which has opened its mouth to receive your brother's blood from your hand. When you work the ground, it shall no longer yield to you its strength. You shall be a fugitive and a wanderer on the earth." Cain said to the Lord, "My punishment is greater than I can bear. Behold, you have driven me today away from the ground, and from your face I shall be hidden. I shall be a fugitive and a wanderer on the earth, and whoever finds me will kill me." Then the Lord said to him, "Not so! If anyone kills Cain, vengeance shall be taken on him sevenfold." And the Lord put a mark on Cain, lest any who found him should attack him. Then Cain went away from the presence of the Lord and settled in the land of Nod, east of Eden.

Cain knew his wife, and she conceived and bore Enoch. When he built a city, he called the name of the city after the name of his son, Enoch. To Enoch was born Irad, and Irad fathered Mehujael, and Mehujael fathered Methushael, and Methushael fathered Lamech. And Lamech took two wives. The name of the one was Adah, and the name of the other Zillah.

Adah bore Jabal; he was the father of those who dwell in tents and have livestock. His brother's name was Jubal; he was the father of all those who play the lyre and pipe. Zillah also bore Tubal-Cain; he was the forger of all instruments of bronze and iron. The sister of Tubal-Cain was Naamah. Lamech said to his wives:

"Adah and Zillah, hear my voice; you wives of Lamech, listen to what I say: I have killed a man for wounding me, a young man for striking me. If Cain's revenge is sevenfold, then Lamech's is seventy-sevenfold."

And Adam knew his wife again, and she bore a son and called his name Seth, for she said, "God has appointed for me another offspring instead of Abel, for Cain killed him." To Seth also a son was born, and he called his name Enosh. At that time people began to call upon the name of the Lord.

Abel and the Christ

The story of Cain and Abel, like the prophecy of Genesis 3, is more than a historical detail. It shows the pattern for human history. Because of sin, the seed of the serpent will choose to glorify itself rather than God, while the seed of the woman will make right relationship with God its deepest desire. Since Cain, the people of the serpent have rejected Yahweh's kingship and oppressed his people who, in a world governed by power and violence, so often seem like failures. Moses draws this out through verse 24 as Cain's offspring build powerful cities and set themselves against God. Cain's treason against God bore fruit in Lamech who called for the same protection God had granted Cain, which only affirmed that evil would have more success in this world than those who are obedient to God.

Just when it seemed that all is lost and wickedness had gained the upper hand against the Creator, God came to Eve to confirm and continue his promise of redemption. As would do throughout history, God gave his people a son. Eve named her son Seth, meaning "God has appointed another son for me." But this son is more than just a son for Eve. Seth is God's guarantee that her seed would continue, would grow, and would one day yield the one seed who would reverse the power of sin in this world when he crushes his enemy's head.

DECEMBER 3

God's Judgment and the Flood

God exiled Adam and Eve from his good government and cast them among the briars and thorns of a lawless world. In killing his brother, Cain had done great evil but broke no laws: no government existed which could arrest him. In the absence of a government, God intervened directly to restore order when he placed a mark on Cain that would protect him from those who might attempt to kill him without fear of consequences. In the absence of laws, however, Abel's murder was just the beginning of anarchy. Humanity's early history regressed from murder to the moral disaster of Noah's age, when everyone did what was right in his own eyes. The world—now outside God's peace, harmony, and bounty—had become the polar-opposite of the garden.

Just nine generations after their expulsion, humans came to see that the curse of Genesis 3 was more than mere words. By rejecting God's kingship, Adam and Eve had plunged the world into moral ruin. Cain and his descendants may have reveled in their freedom from God, but the Scriptures are clear: freedom from God's laws is enslavement to death. By Genesis 9, God decided that he would no longer abide the evil of human anarchy, so he promised to reinstate his gracious rule over a world that human liberty had devastated. God promised to destroy lawlessness and restore justice by unleashing flood waters over the world.

By sending a deluge over the earth, God planned to use the unique character of water to take his creation back to the formless void of Genesis 1:1. The people of the Ancient Near East, who were land-bound, saw water as chaotic and unpredictable. The sea was without form which made it an environment impossible for human beings to inhabit-it was void. And yet desert people valued water, because it was as rare as it was necessary for life. Water also played important cultural roles for people who used it to clean garments, utensils, and their bodies, but also to make preparation for religious rituals. It symbolized both death and life as well as the paradoxical relationship between chaos and cleanliness. When God told Noah about the coming flood waters, he invoked all of water's qualities. He would use the unstoppable power of roiling water to cleanse the world of evil, then, from ground nourished by those same waters, he would grow a new world.

More than execute his justice through the flood, God also established the blueprint of his redemption. His chosen tool for the work of rebuilding the world would be the faith of a man who was known for his loyalty to Yahweh. In a world of anarchy, Noah remained obedient to God's laws. In Genesis 6:9, Moses explains that Noah was not a hero of great strength, but that he was a blameless man. This made Noah unique compared to the heroes of Ancient Near East flood myths, which often portrayed the survivor as a mighty hero who braved the flood waters or stood up to the gods. In the actual story, the hero, Noah, was not a mighty man; he was a man who humbly obeyed God. In order to redeem the world from sin and evil, God would judge his enemies and save his people through the righteousness of a faithful servant.

Noah's role in the great flood was to obey God's instructions about the construction of the ark to the letter, for this ship would protect him and his family from the judgment waters to come. Noah's obedience in a time of God's judgment was not mere historical fact, but a demonstration of God's plan of to redeem all the world back to himself. Human effort is not the agent of redemption, rather God alone destroys evil and restores goodness to the earth as an act of pure grace. God designed the ark, sent the waters, guided the ship, and dried the land—Noah's responsibility was merely to obey God's word. As would be true for all of God's people throughout history, Noah's contribution to redemption was simply to obey God's word, then wait for God to fulfill his promises.

When the flood waters subsided, Noah's steps onto dry land inaugurated a second creation of the world. The first creation was ruined by human sin and unrestrained liberty, but this second creation would be different. Moses explains that God did two things differently after the flood that he had not done before. First, after ridding the earth of lawless evil, God gave the new world a gift that would protect people from the destructive power of anarchy. God created the institution of government when he granted Noah and Noah's descendants the responsibility to kill the one who sheds man's blood. This gift confirmed that human life is precious to God, while it also tasked people to wield governmental power to protect everyone from chaos. In this gift God empowered people to organize into hierarchies and to institute laws by which they could maintain order over the world.

Second, God established a covenant with Noah and Noah's descendants. This was the first time the word covenant appears in the Scriptures. A covenant was a specific kind of legal treaty in which a lord promised his servant protection, while the servant promised to be loyal or obedient. By entering a covenant with all humanity in the second creation, Yahweh made every human life a gift or grant under his protection. The history of this new world would take place beneath the rainbow, a sign of God's guarantee that he would ensure humanity's survival.

But there is more to God's work in Genesis 9 than the institution of government or the establishment of a covenant. For, these two gifts would become the very superstructure of his plan to redeem the world back to himself. The covenant he made with Noah inaugurated a progression of covenants in which God would deepen his relationship with his people, and his world. And the human government God designed would offer more than human protection from great evil, a government under a human king will one day be the power that makes all things new.

GENESIS 9

And God blessed Noah and his sons and said to them, "Be fruitful and multiply and fill the earth. The fear of you and the dread of you shall be upon every beast of the earth and upon every bird of the heavens, upon everything that creeps on the ground and all the fish of the sea. Into your hand they are delivered. Every moving thing that lives shall be food for you. And as I gave you the green plants, I give you everything. But you shall not eat flesh with its life, that is, its blood. And for your lifeblood I will require a reckoning: from every beast I will require it and from man. From his fellow man I will require a reckoning for the life of man.

"Whoever sheds the blood of man, by man shall his blood be shed, for God made man in his own image.

And you, be fruitful and multiply, increase greatly on the earth and multiply in it."

Then God said to Noah and to his sons with him, "Behold, I establish my covenant with you and your offspring after you, and with every living creature that is with you, the birds, the livestock, and every beast of the earth with you, as many as came out of the ark; it is for every beast of the earth. I establish my covenant with you, that never again shall all flesh be cut off by the waters of the flood, and never again shall there be a flood to destroy the earth." And God said, "This is the sign of the covenant that I make between me and you and every living creature that is with you, for all future generations: I have set my bow in the cloud, and it shall be a sign of the covenant between me and the earth. When I bring clouds over the earth and the bow is seen in the clouds, I will remember my covenant that is between me and you and every living creature of all flesh. And the waters shall never again become a flood to destroy all flesh. When the bow is in the clouds, I will see it and remember the everlasting covenant between God and every living creature of all flesh that is on the earth." God said to Noah, "This is the sign of the covenant that I have established between me and all flesh that is on the earth."

The sons of Noah who went forth from the ark were Shem, Ham, and Japheth. (Ham was the father of Canaan.) These three were the sons of Noah, and from these the people of the whole earth were dispersed.

Noah began to be a man of the soil, and he planted a vineyard. He drank of the wine and became drunk and lay uncovered in his tent. And Ham, the father of Canaan, saw the nakedness of his father and told his two brothers outside. Then Shem and Japheth took a garment, laid it on both their shoulders, and walked backward and covered the nakedness of their father. Their faces were turned backward, and they did not see their father's nakedness. When Noah awoke from his wine and knew what his youngest son had done to him, he said,

"Cursed be Canaan.

a servant of servants shall he be to his brothers."
He also said,
"Blessed be the Lord, the God of Shem; and let Canaan be his servant. May God enlarge Japheth, and let him dwell in the tents of Shem, and let Canaan be his servant."
After the flood Noah lived 350 years. All the days of Noah were 950 years, and he died.

Shadows of a Coming King

In Jesus Yahweh lived out the entire story of the flood. Jesus accepts a baptism of water to institute a new cleansing of the body and soul, not by our obedience but by his faithfulness. Through Christ, the better Noah, God recreates not only human relationships to populate his eternal kingdom, but God also restores the full beauty of his entire creation. Christ's work through ministry, death, and resurrection became the fulfillment of all the covenants God made with his people. Jesus became the King of the world, who alone wields the power of life and death in absolute justice so that he might end all chaos, anarchy, and evil. After he completed his task on earth, he ascended to the right hand of the Father to become the head of a human government which will stand as Yahweh's eternal kingdom. And Yahweh established this kingdom when his son, the Christ, offered his own blood to atone for the many ways that, by sinning against Him, Yahweh's people have taken innocent blood. Jesus is the fulfillment of all God promised in the flood and secured through Noah.

DECEMBER 4

The Promise to Abraham

In the cultures of the Ancient Near East, the social reputation of a husband and a wife depended on their ability to have a male child. No matter how successful a person was, if he did not have a son, then his holdings would go to other families at his death. For a woman the stakes were even higher. A woman who bore her husband a son received honor and a place of respect in the community. Many women who did not have sons released their husbands to take surrogate wives so that their families could continue, but such a failure meant a diminished place for the wives. In her day, Sarah's barrenness was a terrible curse—it was the full bloom of sin's terrible seed. While the social implications of barrenness were severe, according to the Scriptures barrenness was also the fleshly consequence of the curse. Life in the garden had been marked by fruitfulness, but life outside of God's rule was precarious and, at times, empty.

God had led Abraham out of his father's country, to the land of promise, but Sarah was still not pregnant. The move seemed to be for nothing. As she aged beyond her childbearing years, Sarah became desperate enough to use the common method of securing a male heir for the family: she gave her maid, Hagar, to her husband. Like every other human effort to bring salvation, the son given to Hagar would bring humanity no closer to restoring its relationship with Yahweh. In Genesis 17, God confirmed that redemption would come by his plan, not Sarah's. Whereas Sarah's plan was a scheme, God promised to fulfill his promise by bringing life out of death. Rather than choose Hagar's fruitful womb, he swore by himself that the lowly and barren wife would give birth to the child who would father a redeeming nation.

God's promise was unlike anything that humanity had envisioned. God would not send armies to march on this broken world or empower a heroic warrior to wreak vengeance on his enemies. Just as he came to a chaotic universe in Genesis 1, so God entered a world which had grown helplessly dark so that he could speak a promise of redemption. To save humanity from their own sin and evil, God promised the birth of a child.

In creation, God chose to bring his goodness to the entire world through the family. He first ordered an otherwise meaningless universe, then cultivated a garden. His command that Adam and Eve be fruitful and multiply would be his plan for extending his reign across the entire globe.

Not only did Adam and Eve reject God's rule when they sinned, Adam and Eve also transformed childbearing into the means by which mankind would cover the world in evil rather than godliness. As human beings after Noah populated the world through sinfulness, God came to Abram with a promise. God would give Abram and his wife a son whose offspring would populate the earth with faithfulness and obedience to God. This new people would one day equal the number of the stars in the sky and the sands on the seashore. By blessing the aging Abraham and Sarah God himself planned to fulfill the command he had given to the first human beings. All this would begin with the birth of a child, a child who would become the father of a godly people.

God had promised that Eve's seed would be the one to conquer humanity's adversary. From the very beginning he had intended that the birth of children would be the vehicle of redemption. That plan seemed to be on the brink of failure since it rested on Sarah, the aging wife of God's chosen servant. God's great work of restoring his world seemed inexorably stuck. The hope of redemption now lay entirely outside of the range of human ability. Neither Abraham nor Sarah had the strength to accomplish the one thing necessary to realize God's plans. For all their ingenuity, intelligence, and determination, they were completely unable to do the one thing they, and all humans, so desperately needed.

Since the fall, all people have toiled away in a broken world, helpless to save themselves. But God brings life out of death so that he alone is its redeemer.

GENESIS 12:1–9, 17:15–27

Now the Lord said to Abram, "Go from your country and your kindred and your father's house to the land that I will show you. And I will make of you a great nation, and I will bless you and make your name great, so that you will be a blessing. I will bless those who bless you, and him who dishonors you I will curse, and in you all the families of the earth shall be blessed."

So, Abram went, as the Lord had told him, and Lot went with him. Abram was seventy-five years old when he departed from Haran. And Abram took Sarai his wife, and Lot his brother's son, and all their possessions that they had gathered, and the people that they had acquired in Haran, and they set out to go to the land of Canaan. When they came to the land of Canaan, Abram passed through the land to the place at Shechem, to the oak of Moreh. At that time the Canaanites were in the land. Then the Lord appeared to Abram and said, "To your offspring I will give this land." So, he built there an altar to the Lord, who had appeared to him. From there he moved to the hill country on the east of Bethel and pitched his tent, with Bethel on the west and Ai on the east. And there he built an altar to the Lord and called upon the name of the Lord. And Abram journeyed on, still going toward the Negeb.

And God said to Abraham, "As for Sarai your wife, you shall not call her name Sarai, but Sarah shall be her name. I will bless her, and moreover, I will give you a son by her. I will bless her, and she shall become nations; kings of peoples shall come from her." Then Abraham fell on his face and laughed and said to himself, "Shall a child be born to a man who is a hundred years old? Shall Sarah, who is ninety years old, bear a child?" And Abraham said to God, "Oh that Ishmael might live before you!" God said, "No, but Sarah your wife shall bear you a son, and you shall call his name Isaac. I will establish my covenant with him as an everlasting covenant for his offspring after him. As for Ishmael, I have heard you; behold, I have blessed him and will make him fruitful and multiply him greatly. He shall father twelve princes, and I will make him into a great nation. But I will establish my covenant with Isaac, whom Sarah shall bear to you at this time next year."

When he had finished talking with him, God went up from Abraham. Then Abraham took Ishmael his son and all those born in his house or bought with his money, every male among the men of Abraham's house, and he circumcised the flesh of their foreskins that very day, as God had said to him. Abraham was ninety-nine years old when he was circumcised in the flesh of his foreskin. And Ishmael his son was thirteen years old when he was circumcised in the flesh of his foreskin. That very day Abraham and his son Ishmael were circumcised. And all the men of his house, those born in the house and those bought with money from a foreigner, were circumcised with him.

God Has Given Us a Son

Israel's unfaithfulness and disloyalty to God in Canaan, the promised land, was the second fall of mankind. In turning to idols, and other proscribed fruit, the Israelites squandered life under the perfect reign of king Yahweh. God exiled them from the promised land to work among the thorns and thistles of foreign governments. By their own efforts the kingdom of God could not be restored. Their strength failed. Into the darkness of their oppression their Redeemer spoke a new promise not unlike the one he spoke to their forefather, Abraham. The promise fit the pattern with which Israel should have been familiar: God swore he would create a people that would cover the earth, a people that he would call out from every nation and tongue. This awesome promise hinged on the birth of a son. Like his choice of Sarah, God would fulfill this promise through a womb made barren by her virginity. In this God promised a miracle as impossible as creating a nation through the womb of a woman beyond childbearing age. On the birth of that child all the world's hope for redemption, rest, and restoration would hinge.

DECEMBER 5

All the Nations Will be the Lord's

The wisdom of the world seems right to those who have accepted their exile. Israelites who were dragged from their homeland felt the sting of God's judgment as they mourned the loss of their identities. But when they forgot what they had really lost, they forgot that they were in exile. Homes, food, communities, and protection could be found in any human city, but the presence of Yahweh could not. Israel had not just been the Hebrew's national home, but it was, most importantly, where God chose to dwell. Alienated from him, the Israelites would never be home, but as they forgot God, they fell into the danger of accepting exile as their normal condition. Even as the Israelites sought to return to their homeland, they failed to recognize that what they needed most was not defensive walls or a Hebrew government. They needed to be restored to God.

The garden into which God placed Adam and Eve was good in every way. Under his reign humanity had everything. When Adam and Eve were faced with the harsh reality of thorns and thistles, God promised that by his own work he would one day end mankind's exile in order to bring it back under his good government. But this plan would take a great deal of time, and so God counseled not only Adam and Eve but all his people to wait for his restoration. This command to wait was not a call to passiveness, but to active obedience to God while in exile.

But obeying God while waiting on Him has always proven difficult for his people. In his absence humans become impatient. They often attempt to bring their own idea of order to the fallen world, not in anticipation of God's coming kingdom but rather in place of it. They establish governments, constructed economies, and pass laws, all designed to make this world a home under their own control. They have developed technological advances to improve life and used creativity to make their surroundings beautiful. While people imitate their Creator in all these things, humans have mistakenly believed that their creative powers can transform this world into a paradise, rather than look through this world to see their relationship with God as their only true need and desire.

By making this world their home, people have explicitly or implicitly rejected God's kingdom. After the flood, God's people built the tower of Babel to establish a home that would allow them to forget they were in exile. In the same way, some of those who would later be taken captive by the Babylonians or Assyrians became comfortable with their lives away from Jerusalem. Returning home to a broken city and a broken temple may have felt more like traveling to a foreign land than going home.

This picture of exile is, at the very least, a helpful metaphor for the universal human condition. Our exile since the fall has been marked by more than the thorns and thistles of the cursed soil. Death has invaded every part of the human experience, and yet people have learned to accept death, suffering, and difficulty. We have invented ways of explaining these things without having to admit that we are in exile. In the ancient period, nations developed understandings of the gods which allowed them to see death as a normal part of their own lives. So, too, in the modern period, we accept the ugliness of our exile from God's garden by making life comfortable and rationalizing death as the natural culmination of life.

The human tendency to pretend that our world is our home and that living in God's good kingdom would be exile from this world is not merely a mindless habit. For the love of this world has caused people not only to grow comfortable here but also to cultivate an abiding hatred of God. Rather than recognize that life in this world is exile from him, they accuse God of threatening their gardens and rage against his authority. So far from seeing love for God as new life, they consider it, perversely, to be death. They do not see the law of God as freedom from the diseased grip of sin, but as slavery. Ultimately, the world embraces a spiritual unreality with a kind of whole-hearted emotional conviction. The nations of this world believe that they inhabit the only home there is, and they deride God's people for accepting a self-imposed exile from their worldly gardens.

The Scriptures often refer to humanity's love of exile as a blindness. People think that what they see in their cultures or what they value in their man-made habitats is all there is. Because they are unable to see this world as broken, sinful people have no more ability to imagine God's eternal kingdom than a person born blind can imagine the shape of a mountain or the colors of a desert sunset. People need the Holy Spirit to show them what is real. Yahweh's kingdom is the only true and perfect kingdom, and it is not of this world—all people must wait to be brought home while they live here in exile.

But God is not willing to forfeit the nations of this world to their own blindness. In his garden, the true home of humanity, God called for Adam and Eve to be fruitful, multiply, and cover the earth. In fact, the nations have inadvertently been doing what God ordered even though they have been doing so in service to their own ambitions. In mercy God has given them a season to build their own gardens, but by his own timing he will bring them all into his kingdom. Nothing can stop Yahweh from spreading his reign and rule across this entire globe so that its every corner comes under his command.

The reality is this: the world will once again be the garden of the Lord and, Scripture tells us, by the time God assumes direct and full command of this world, his beautiful garden will have matured into a heavenly city.

The reversal of human exile will not be a natural, historical event. Humans who have determined that they are already home in this fallen world will fight to protect what they have. Thus, in order to restore his government, Yahweh will destroy the plans of human governments and then judge those who have set themselves against him. He constructed the model of his own rule by giving mankind governments and kings, but in the restoration of his kingdom Yahweh will dethrone all the earth's rulers and reclaim their broken nations. God himself will accomplish this glorious plan by his own power and without human aid. Indeed, God has not been silent about his plan. He has graciously revealed this plan to the nations so they might turn from their rage against his King, admit their lostness, and, like the prodigal son, come home in humble repentance and obedience.

PSALM 2

Why do the nations rage and the peoples plot in vain? The kings of the earth set themselves, and the rulers take counsel together, against the Lord and against his Anointed, saying,

"Let us burst their bonds apart and cast away their cords from us."

He who sits in the heavens laughs; the Lord holds them in derision. Then he will speak to them in his wrath, and terrify them in his fury, saying, "As for me, I have set my King on Zion, my holy hill."

I will tell of the decree:

The Lord said to me, "You are my Son; today I have begotten you.

Ask of me, and I will make the nations your heritage, and the ends of the earth your possession. You shall break them with a rod of iron and dash them in pieces like a potter's vessel."

Now therefore, O kings, be wise; be warned, O rulers of the earth. Serve the Lord with fear and rejoice with trembling.

Kiss the Son, lest he be angry, and you perish in the way, for his wrath is quickly kindled. Blessed are all who take refuge in him.

The King of All the Nations

According to Paul in Philippians 2, Jesus willfully and lovingly joined humanity in its exile when he was born as a baby on Christmas morning. He left the glorious realm of his Father's perfect reign so that he might subject himself to the injustices of human life.

By the world's standards Jesus was a poor leader. He entered the world through an impoverished family so that he might comfort an oppressed people. While this made little sense to the Jews and was lunacy to the Greeks, it fit the grand plan of restoration Yahweh promised in Genesis 3. Christ did not come to the seed of the serpent, in all Satan's power, but rather to those who knew they were in exile to proclaim to them that their exile was nearing its end. He preached the kingdom of God so that his people might know that in this life they live estranged from their true home, that they might return home to him through repentance not human effort. In this way Jesus, the Son of God, undercut all the earthly claims of human governments. For, the Good News he preached in his brief time on earth, he lived out in his resurrection. Like Moses, who led Israel out of exile in Egypt, Christ has established the road by which he will lead us in an exodus from our own exile, through the waters of death, and into the home he has prepared for us, a home in which we will live with him and under his reign forever.

THE TEMPLE

Eden, the paradise God created for Adam and Eve, and the New Jerusalem, the future kingdom of Christ in Revelation 22, are both defined by the same reality: God lives with his people. The natural world and human society may be great wonders, but they are pale and broken without their Creator. According to the Scriptures, God created the world to serve as his home. He is both its beauty and its meaning.

Humans better understand God's relationship to his creation when they imitate him. God made humans in his image so that they, like him, can think, create, and love. As we build buildings, compose music, and care for our neighbors, we come to understand something deeper about God's relationship to his creation. Our creations are meaningful long after their authors have departed. We still appreciate Michelangelo's sculptures centuries after his death. In true creation, however, what has been made cannot exist without the one who made it. More than that, the creation cannot be complete without its maker. Created beings are not whole, they are not able finally to discover meaning without being in personal relationship with their Creator. In Genesis 1, God walks with Adam and Eve. In Revelation 22, humanity has no need of any other warmth or light than its loving Creator.

We often measure the effects of sin and the fall in terms of human suffering, but this metric is only a symptom of the great ugliness which now defines our world. Sin forced a chasm between the world and its holy Creator, and that chasm became the source of all our pain. At the beginning, the universe shared in the moral perfection of its maker; it was the holy habitation of a holy God. Sin, however, defiled not just the human heart but the place which God had made for himself. To save his creation God removed himself in some personal way from all that he made, taking with himself the only source of peace, health, and goodness. We are alienated from our Creator, our lives no longer defined by his love but by death—the terrible, unavoidable destination of our lives. God made the order needed for life; sin brought disorder that leads to death. Having broken God's word, Adam and Eve entered a broken world as broken people who would begin to die.

Although God removed himself from his creation because of sin, he did not abandon humanity to its own hopeless devices. From the moment that he exiled humanity from the garden he began the only story that has ever been told—by entering into a relationship with his people, God will bring meaning, purpose, and life back to his creation. He will redeem a broken world when he comes to live in his creation and among his people once more. This is the longing of every human heart, the tune of every song humanity has ever written, and the plot of every book ever written. People have always known that they are meaningful, but they have not been able to discover exactly what that meaning is. They have built cultures and societies to craft purpose for themselves, even though the meaning they seek belongs only to Yahweh. Moses seems to explore the tragedy of the human search for meaning in his description of life after the fall and of the construction of the great tower called Babel.

Without God, the human search for purpose and meaning devolved into absolute evil just a few generations after the fall from Eden. To restore his place in his family, Cain alienated himself from God, which led him to become history's first murderer. From this point on, humanity descended into filth. People not only rejected their Creator but by doing so they mangled the beauty and goodness that remained in God's world. Through the waters of the flood God cleansed the earth of human evil. Then, out of the world's wreckage he saved Noah, the man with whom he had an intimate relationship. From that relationship God planned to rebuild his creation. Rather than follow Noah's example, however, humanity set out on an ambitious plan that was quite opposite to the days of Noah, although just as ill-fated.

According to Moses in Genesis 11, humanity did not descend into lawlessness but rather decided to assert its own order over the world in a historic building project. Noah's descendants built a mighty tower that proved to be humanity's most successful society in the history of the world. It was a building of technical genius produced by a state of such peace and harmony; it may be that no other people in history have been able to match its genius. By human standards Babel was a paradise that rivaled Eden. But God saw in humanity's unrivaled success an evil as dangerous as anarchy—idolatry. Babel was a godless city. Its architects built a society not to restore their relationship with God, but to make life on this earth perfect without him. Idolatry is the effort to succeed in service to anything or anyone other than Yahweh, who is the only source of all goodness. Rather than allow the idolatry of Babel to metastasize, God broke its citizens' language. He judged the human desire to live without him, then set in motion a plan to build a different city. This city would have Yahweh as its builder, as its king, as its capital. God's city would have at its heart a building very different than a tower of human genius. God planned a building that would be the first step in his plan to fully return to his universe. He put in motion the plan to build the temple.

In Genesis 12, God called Abraham out of Ur of the Chaldeans to go to a land that he would tell him. This command was more than a new direction for a man and his family. Rather it was the inauguration of a plan to build a house for himself in the world. This house would become for all humanity the hope of new life and the destruction of death. To live among his people, God would have to engineer a space which, by his own design, would be holy so that a holy God could occupy it. As Moses was writing the story of God's plan to make Abraham into the nation of his presence, he was experiencing just a foretaste of this promise. He was meeting with God behind a veil in the tent of meeting. From these meetings Moses penned both the law, which became the order of a new humanity, as well as the story of how God would finally re-create all things. Through Moses God advanced his redemptive plan.

Israel was defined by this tent. In carrying it with them, they carried the hope of all the world. God first visited his people in the ark of the covenant in the tent of meeting. But once Israel had conquered the land of Canaan, he commanded that a temple be built. This temple would be a stable home for God, a home that all humanity could locate. God crafted it to be a space of escalating holiness, from outer chambers into the holy of holies. Only the high priest who had followed every one of God's meticulous instructions could enter. The rest of Israel, the rest of humanity, could only stand outside, but they knew that their God resided in the middle of their city. Israel understood the significance of the temple. All of life revolved around its calendar and worship. Law flowed from its porticos, protection from its power, and identity from its beauty.

While the temple made it possible for Israel to live with God, the people again gave in to the lies of idolatry. They sought fulfillment in other gods, in ways of life other than God's way. As Israel betrayed Yahweh, it became apparent that the temple was not meant to be the final stage of God's plan. All of history pointed to the time when he would dwell with his people, but because of their sin he could no longer live in the temple. He departed Jerusalem and purged the land. But he swore he would not abandon his promise to live with his people. The nation of Israel failed to serve as his holy home, so he told of a time when he would come to all people. Like the holy of holies, the space in which he would live would have to be morally perfect. As sacrifices performed by priests once purified Israel so that God could live in his people's midst, so a sacrifice would have to purify all people.

The apostle John shook the very foundations of this broken world when he wrote of Jesus Christ, that "the Word became flesh and dwelt among us." (John 1:14) The word for "dwelt" is best translated, "tabernacled."

DECEMBER 6

The Son of Promise

Isaac was the son of promise. God planned to rescue his people from their exile through the gift of childbirth. From the beginning he promised to save the world through Eve's children, and their progeny, even though Scripture records that her line of descendants was dangerously thin at times. For example, among Seth's descendants Noah seemed to be the only seed of the woman still obedient to God. During Abraham's life, however, the line seemed to have stopped altogether. As Abraham and Sarah aged beyond their childbearing years and still did not have a son, all hope seemed lost. Year after year, God called the aging couple to trust him and to wait.

God had given them his word, but Abraham and Sarah gave up on him at times. As Abraham traveled through foreign lands, he claimed that his beautiful wife was his sister so that leaders would not kill him to gain Sarah. In these moments Abraham lost trust in Yahweh and, reasoning that his line would not continue if he was dead, he took matters into his own hands. Abraham may have ensured his own survival, but by giving Sarah to other men he allowed others to have children through her. Later Sarah herself made the same mistake by allowing Abraham to have a child through Hagar as a last-ditch effort to secure a son for their future and so fulfill God's promise on her terms. The long wait cracked their faith in Yahweh, and they lost hope. Despite their many failures, however, God graciously preserved them. He rescued Sarah from the local kings and then, by miracle, gave Sarah a son, Isaac. God blessed them despite their weak faith.

Through the birth of Isaac, Abraham and Sarah became the agents of God's redemptive work, but they also served another purpose. God revealed through them the ways that he would complete his redemptive work. First, God redeems his people purely by a grace that he works through the brokenness of his people. Jacob, Joseph's brothers, the Hebrews, Moses, David, and Solomon—just to mention a few—failed to trust God's plan. Despite the weaknesses of his people, God did not abandon them. We can learn this one lesson from the story of God's redemption—he redeems his people by his grace and power alone despite their broken faith.

Second, Yahweh calls his people to the trials of waiting on him for salvation. God could have granted the couple a child during their younger years if he had so desired. But he delayed, and through Abraham and Sarah, God taught his people that trusting in him always comes with painful waiting. God did not establish Eve's seed until after she endured Abel's death and Cain's banishment. Insufferable days, months, and years passed before God granted to Eve a son. Noah, his family, and the animals remained on the ark for over a year as God raised, then lowered the waters of judgment. The Scriptures record that nearly six months of floating on raging storm waters passed before, as Moses records it, "God remembered Noah." God does not forget his people, but his people often feel forgotten. The writer of the Hebrews explains that at the root and foundation of God's work of redemption is the faith of his people. This faith is not blind belief, but rather an active trust in God that overcomes the long, dark, lonely waiting for his redemption.

As Isaac grew into a young man, Abraham and Sarah witnessed the power of God's faithfulness contrasted against their faithlessness. They repeatedly jeopardized Yahweh's redemptive plan, but he fulfilled his promises through them nonetheless. Through their trials and failures, God accomplished many things, but maybe the most important was that he perfected their faith by tempering their trust. He also granted them a vision of his redemption which they would hand down to their descendants. He revealed that through their faith God planned to redeem all of creation. God would call all his people to the task of serving him in a broken world as they awaited the realization of his kingdom on earth. It is a wonder that God would realize the greatest hopes of all humanity through the broken faith of a few sinful individuals. Abraham and Sarah did more than learn this: they lived it, modeled it, and passed it down to God's people as the way of life in his kingdom.

The trials that Abraham and Sarah had endured, however, paled in comparison to Abraham's final trial. In Genesis 22, God himself called Abraham to do the one thing that would destroy not only his future but the hope of all humanity. The world's redemption hinged on the life of the boy whom God now called Abraham to sacrifice, the one and only son of promise. In previous experiences Abraham had trusted himself for survival rather than God. God now put him to the test—would he trust himself and run from God, or trust God and sacrifice his only son?

The trial must have been excruciating. Along the terrible road to Mount Moriah, Abraham waited every night for a new command from God. He must have looked for any sign that God was only bluffing. God did not speak; Abraham did not turn back. For three terrible days Abraham walked the most painful path any human could walk. And yet, step by step he lived out a faith that would characterize all of God's people, for he believed that God would keep his promises even if doing so seemed impossible. Abraham trusted God above everything that existed either inside or outside himself. In response to this deep faith, God stopped Abraham from completing the sacrifice and provided a ram to serve as Isaac's substitute. The ram not only saved Isaac's life, but it also saved Abraham from doing what he most feared to do. More than that, by becoming the sacrifice in Isaac's stead, the ram fulfilled God's promise to make of Abraham the nation through which he would restore the world.

GENESIS 22:1–19

After these things God tested Abraham and said to him, "Abraham!" And he said, "Here I am." He said, "Take your son, your only son Isaac, whom you love, and go to the land of Moriah, and offer him there as a burnt offering on one of the mountains of which I shall tell you." So Abraham rose early in the morning, saddled his donkey, and took two of his young men with him, and his son Isaac. And he cut the wood for the burnt offering and arose and went to the place of which God had told him. On the third day Abraham lifted up his eyes and saw the place from afar. Then Abraham said to his young men, "Stay here with the donkey; I and the boy will go over there and worship and come again to you." And Abraham took the wood of the burnt offering and laid it on Isaac his son. And he took in his hand the fire and the knife. So they went both of them together. And Isaac said to his father Abraham, "My father!" And he said, "Here I am, my son." He said, "Behold, the fire and the wood, but where is the lamb for a burnt offering?" Abraham said, "God will provide for himself the lamb for a burnt offering, my son." So they went both of them together.

When they came to the place of which God had told him, Abraham built the altar there and laid the wood in order and bound Isaac his son and laid him on the altar, on top of the wood. Then Abraham reached out his hand and took the knife to slaughter his son. But the angel of the Lord called to him from heaven and said, "Abraham, Abraham!" And he said, "Here I am." He said, "Do not lay your hand on the boy or do anything to him, for now I know that you fear God, seeing you have not withheld your son, your only son, from me." And Abraham lifted up his eyes and looked, and behold, behind him was a ram, caught in a thicket by his horns. And Abraham went and took the ram and offered it up as a burnt offering instead of his son. So Abraham called the name of that place, "The Lord will provide"; as it is said to this day, "On the mount of the Lord it shall be provided."

And the angel of the Lord called to Abraham a second time from heaven and said, "By myself I have sworn, declares the Lord, because you have done this and have not withheld your son, your only son, I will surely bless you, and I will surely multiply your offspring as the stars of heaven and as the sand that is on the seashore. And your offspring shall possess the gate of his enemies, and in your offspring shall all the nations of the earth be blessed, because you have obeyed my voice." So Abraham returned to his young men, and they arose and went together to Beersheba. And Abraham lived at Beersheba.

Jesus the King of Promise

Jesus Christ was the better Isaac: not only was Christ the son of promise, but he is also the king who God promised to his people since the beginning. All the descendants of Seth lived and had children for the birth of this one seed of Eve. He was the king who would bring all his people back to his Father. All the hopes of humanity rested on this one child. God the Father spoke of Christ in Genesis 3 when he said that the seed of the woman would crush Satan's head. But the seed of the woman must suffer a bruised heel first. Adam and Eve must have wondered what this meant, but God the Father knew exactly what it meant. To redeem his people, Yahweh must sacrifice his own son on a wooden altar. But this terrible event did not happen that day, week, or even century. Yahweh did not endure a three-day walk; he waited for thousands of years for the day when he would walk his son out of the camp and onto a desolate hill.

The faith of Abraham was only a rough and shaky shadow of the faithfulness of his God, who would not be spared killing his own son. For Jesus would be both the child of promise and the sacrificial ram. Through him God would realize all his promises, for Jesus would be the sacrifice once and for all for his people's sin so that he might become the king of a new creation.

DECEMBER 7

The Ladder to God

At times in history the promises of God to restore his world seemed to hang on the thoughtless decisions of spoiled children. In one instance, Isaac's youngest son, Jacob, tricked Isaac into giving him the blessing meant for Esau, the firstborn son. A father's blessing in the ancient world confirmed the oldest son's role as the head of the family upon the father's death. But the blessing of Isaac meant more than just familial headship because God had promised to make Abraham a great nation through Isaac and Isaac's heir, Esau. At his mother's urging, however, Jacob had covered himself in wool and altered his voice so that his then blind father would think he was blessing Esau. Jacob's deceitful actions had serious implications for his father's entire family and estate, but given Isaac's place in God's plans, his actions also had cosmic ramifications.

Jacob's lie created a crisis. Esau was not only the true older son, but he was also a strong and virile man. The Scriptures make it clear that Jacob was slight of stature and not used to the physical demands of outdoor labor and hunting. Esau, on the other hand, was a rugged man who had been tempered by hard work. Jacob's only chance of enjoying his father's blessing was avoiding a fight with his older brother, a fight that he could not win.

Hoping to protect her beloved son from Esau's rage, Rebekah warned Jacob to flee to her brother Laban's house as she waited for the day that Esau would forget what Jacob had done. Once it was safe for Jacob to return, she would call for him to come home, but until that day Jacob would be in exile. Before he left, Isaac called Jacob and gave him some instructions for his journey. The first was a request that Jacob take a wife from his own people. The second was a prayer that God would not only grow Isaac's family, but that God would confer to him all of Abraham's blessings. With that, Jacob fled from his father's tent into the wilderness and began the long, lonely journey away from his familiar home.

Jacob left his father and began his five-hundred-mile trek to his uncle's estate in Haran. He walked north, parallel to the Dead Sea and then the Jordan River for about sixty miles when he decided to stop and sleep. During the night Jacob had a dream that altered his reality: he saw a vision of a ladder that stretched from the ground on which he slept to the very heavens. The shocking part of his dream was not a ladder that crossed the physical distance between Earth and the celestial spaces but rather a ladder that connected the perfect kingdom of the Holy God to a broken world. In Genesis 11, humanity had pooled all its genius and resources to accomplish this task. Rather than reaching heaven, mankind only succeeded in creating a kingdom that opposed its God and so faced his righteous judgment.

But here on a hill in Palestine, God built a very different structure that did not begin on earth but rather reached down from his glorious realm to Earth—a structure meant not for habitation, but as a conduit that carried God's messengers. God pulled the curtain away for a moment to show Jacob that his promises were not mere words but a spiritual and physical reality. His spoken promises materialized into an actual movement of angelic agents who would bring to fulfillment all that he said.

Since the judgment of Babel, God had been making clear that his promise of restoration would not happen by the will or work of mankind. Jacob's lie seemed to have thwarted God's promises, but in reality, no such thing could happen. God was going to bring about his plan through Jacob, despite Jacob. God's words at the end of the vision make this clear. God will do what he has promised to do. The vision was larger than Jacob could even fathom. For him, in that moment, it confirmed that he would be the one through whom God would fulfill his promises. Jacob would become the head of his father's family and his children would become the nation which God had foretold.

But the promise was greater than Jacob could have imagined. God not only confirmed Jacob's place in his plan, but he also revealed what that plan would be. God would open a new connection between the realm of his reign and the realm of this world. The ladder spoke of a new reality, the very real condescension of God from his perfect kingdom to the world of sinful people. This was not a promise of mere physical or economic bounty, but the hope of a restored relationship between Jacob's descendants and God himself. God alone inaugurated this redeeming work with no help from Jacob, who simply watched the miracle of God's love unfold before him.

GENESIS 28:10–22

Jacob left Beersheba and went toward Haran. And he came to a certain place and stayed there that night, because the sun had set. Taking one of the stones of the place, he put it under his head and lay down in that place to sleep. And he dreamed, and behold, there was a ladder set up on the earth, and the top of it reached to heaven. And behold, the angels of God were ascending and descending on it! And behold, the Lord stood above it and said, "I am the Lord, the God of Abraham your father and the God of Isaac. The land on which you lie I will give to you and to your offspring. Your offspring shall be like the dust of the earth, and you shall spread abroad to the west and to the east and to the north and to the south, and in you and your offspring shall all the families of the earth be blessed. Behold, I am with you and will keep you wherever you go and will bring you back to this land. For I will not leave you until I have done what I have promised you." Then Jacob awoke from his sleep and said, "Surely the Lord is in this place, and I did not know it." And he was afraid and said, "How awesome is this place! This is none other than the house of God, and this is the gate of heaven."

So early in the morning Jacob took the stone that he had put under his head and set it up for a pillar and poured oil on the top of it. He called the name of that place Bethel, but the name of the city was Luz at the first. Then Jacob made a vow, saying, "If God will be with me and will keep me in this way that I go, and will give me bread to eat and clothing to wear, so that I come again to my father's house in peace, then the Lord shall be my God, and this stone, which I have set up for a pillar, shall be God's house. And of all that you give me I will give a full tenth to you."

The True Way to Yahweh

Humanity has, in all times and all places, sought the road that leads back to its Creator, but its greatest efforts have only led it into spiritual cul-de-sacs in this fallen world. By the time of the first century, in the Mediterranean world, the Jews themselves had turned the Torah into an instruction manual for building an earthly kingdom. The greatest power of the day, Rome, had built a world-conquering military as it subjugated barbarian cultures under the civilizing power of imperial laws. Revolutionaries and practitioners of mystery religions, while they were marginalized, practiced magical rituals to resist political oppression in this life.

But Jesus came into the world to show a more excellent way. Against the dead ends which frustrated this world's greatest ambitions, Jesus declared that "I am the way the truth and the life, no one comes to the father but by me." (John 14:6) He did not claim to be the way toward utopia in this world but rather the only way to the Creator. But his exclusive claim was the most gracious claim ever uttered by a human tongue. For God did not wait for humanity to build a ladder that could reach to the heavens; rather he became the ladder himself. He reached from his perfect realm of splendor unimaginable to this broken world, so that he might be the flesh and bone upon which we travel back to our Father.

DECEMBER 8

All the Nations

While God has judged humanity for sinning against its Creator, he has not abandoned humanity. Many people have misunderstood the Old Testament as the half of the Bible that describes a God of judgment who destroys enemies and punishes his people without compassion. To say this is to misunderstand the real weight and power of both the Old and New Testaments. In truth, while Israel deserved to be finally rejected by God, he did not abandon his people to their own sin. He had every reason to repay hate with hate, to consign humanity to servility to idols, then to the bondage of the grave. But God initiated his relationship with Abraham and then Israel of his own accord. He started the process by which he would rescue a humanity that despised being rescued. And though God judged evil in a very physical way, he often did so to show the real weight of human sin and the true gulf between people and their Creator. But God even did these acts in service to his deep love for his people and his gracious plan to redeem all things back to himself.

God called his people out of a broken and sinful world so that they might live for their king, the author of life. To modern people, a king is an antiquated political figure who wielded power unaccountably and therefore unjustly. But for ancient peoples, the king was more than a person of illegitimate power; he was, in some sense, the father of the people. The bond between the king and his subjects was not a bond of mere subjugation, but a bond of love. The king would take the first position in battles against enemies and use the lavish riches of the kingdom to adorn the people's glory. While the role of king was an image easily at hand in the ancient period, it is foreign to us now. We see governments only as good when they are held accountable and tend to think of them as dispassionate systems that incorporate laws, police, and infrastructure to direct society. But this notion had no place in the culture surrounding the sons of Korah.

For the writers of the psalms, God was the true and ultimate king of all people and all nations, even though all people have rejected him and his rightful rule. People not only ignore their Creator, according to the Scriptures, but by nature they hate their Creator. They choose idols or the strength of horses rather than trust Yahweh. It is this hatred for their true king that is the seed of all human evil—from slander and gossip to adultery and murder. The opposite is also true: right relationship with God is the starting point for all right relationships between people. In Scripture the relationship between Yahweh, the King, and his people is the animating force of all loving relationships, such as those between friends, and even spouses. Inversely, this means that the beauty of human relationships teaches us, in simple ways, the dimensions of God's love which make those relationships possible.

Humans have a difficult time understanding the love that God has for his people and in turn do not know how to conceptualize what their love for God should be. The Scriptures do not lack such imagination, for the Bible portrays God not only as judge or redeemer but also as king, husband, shepherd, and father. This means that the complex dimensions of human life are not random accidents. Rather, God crafted human relationships to help us understand him better. When seen this way, we understand that God made human beings, and all the world, to serve as his base vocabulary for knowing who he is. The breathless beauty of the earth serves as a window into his mind and genius. The scale of the universe gives us a way to measure our awe of him. The differences in gender teach us the balance of his personality. And human love opens a door to a fathomless arena of joy, tenderness, care, meaning, fulfillment, and purpose that God alone can plumb. The example of earthly kingship is one of the Scriptures' primary pictures for defining the relationship between Yahweh and his people.

Modern, Western people often associate kings with abuse and illegitimate privilege. Israel, however, would have understood that the king was the person who defined the life of the people. In the Ancient Near East, the king was the head of the people as the husband was the head of the household. The moral character of the people followed from the character of the king, even though all historical kings, as humans, have suffered from moral corruption. Despite the sin of human kings, however, God created the office of king in human history so that the people of Israel would better understand who he was. For Israel, all human kings were temporary stand-ins for Yahweh. He is the true and noble king who leads his people into peace, who disciplines his people to correct their character, and leads the fight against his people's true enemies.

God wove into human life the threads which we must use to tie together our understanding of him. The leadership of kings, which serves as the framework even for romantic love between a man and a woman, was given by God as a simple expression of what our finite hearts are too small to grasp. In the complex relationship between a king and his people, and in the passion of the marital bond, God has left us shadows of an affection that is so deep that only the Holy Spirit can express through sounds what words cannot capture.

PSALM 45

My heart overflows with a pleasing theme; I address my verses to the king; my tongue is like the pen of a ready scribe.

You are the most handsome of the sons of men; grace is poured upon your lips; therefore God has blessed you forever. Gird your sword on your thigh, O mighty one, in your splendor and majesty!

In your majesty ride out victoriously for the cause of truth and meekness and righteousness; let your right hand teach you awesome deeds! Your arrows are sharp in the heart of the king's enemies; the peoples fall under you.

Your throne, O God, is forever and ever.

The scepter of your kingdom is a scepter of uprightness; you have loved righteousness and hated wickedness. Therefore God, your God, has anointed you with the oil of gladness beyond your companions; your robes are all fragrant with myrrh and aloes and cassia. From ivory palaces stringed instruments make you glad; daughters of kings are among your ladies of honor; at your right hand stands the queen in gold of Ophir.

Hear, O daughter, and consider, and incline your ear: forget your people and your father's house, and the king will desire your beauty.

Since he is your lord, bow to him.

The people of Tyre will seek your favor with gifts, the richest of the people.

All glorious is the princess in her chamber, with robes interwoven with gold.

In many-colored robes she is led to the king, with her virgin companions following behind her. With joy and gladness, they are led along as they enter the palace of the king.

In place of your fathers shall be your sons; you will make
them princes in all the earth.

I will cause your name to be remembered in all generations;
therefore, nations will praise you forever and ever.

King of All the Nations

The Jews rejected Jesus. John was clear in the beginning of his
Gospel that Jesus came to his own people, to his own subjects, but
they knew him not. Unlike ancient peoples who suffered under
unjust rulers, Jesus, the king, accepted the violence done to him by
an unjust people. It is terribly ironic that it took the pagan, Roman
proconsul to realize who Christ was when he sincerely asked, "Are
you a king?" A king, no ... *the* King, yes.

During his ministry Jesus explored the depth of this truth with
his disciples. Through parables and teachings, Jesus described
himself as the true shepherd who leads, disciplines, protects, and
dies for his sheep. He used the metaphor of a vineyard owner
who entrusted his servants with his wealth, and a master who
empowered his servants to be productive and faithful. Throughout
his teaching, Jesus spoke most often about the kingdom of heaven,
because through his own actions he was redeeming the human
understanding of a king. His holiness directs the sanctification of
his people, while his sacrifice and love remake his people's hearts.
He is the animating force of all noble human relationships—the
one who makes love, love. It is Christ for whom all the nations
yearn; they are all restless until they find their rest in their true,
eternal king.

DECEMBER 9

No Life Outside of Yahweh

In Exodus 7, Moses presented himself to Pharaoh as the emissary of a mighty king. Moses warned Pharaoh that the king he represented would invade Egypt, destroy its gods and its defenses, then slaughter the heir to the throne if Pharaoh did not turn the Hebrews over to their true king. Rather than capitulate to King Yahweh, Pharaoh opposed the Hebrews' monarch and so joined a war he had no chance of winning. Through the words and staff of Moses, Yahweh defeated Egypt's gods, stripped the country of its plenty, killed Pharaoh's heir, and destroyed Egypt's mighty army. He rescued his people with an awesome display of power—there has never been a king like Yahweh. After he led his people across the Red Sea and out of Egypt, Moses, his chosen representative, sang out a national hymn of praise to his mighty king.

But the Hebrews struggled to understand that Yahweh was a king who was different from every other king. Unlike the rulers of other nations, Yahweh led his people from the rich lush farmlands of the Nile flood basin into desert wastes. Instead of fields speckled with sheep, cattle, and barley, King Yahweh dropped manna in the sand and quail in the brush, day after day. Rather than settle in a homeland, his people wandered in wastelands. By the world's normal standards for a king, Yahweh was a failure. When the Hebrews finally arrived at Sinai, Moses disappeared into smoke and thunder while the people lived in tents on meager rations. They lost hope in their new sovereign and rejected his emissary.

Of course, Yahweh had been clear about his reign from the very beginning. He demanded that Pharaoh allow his people to go into the desert not to start a rival power in the Sinai, but to worship their God. Thus, his people's time in the desert was not a sign of Yahweh's failure but rather his plan to teach the Hebrews about being the people of a holy God. Human rulers use power to acquire land and secure milk and honey for their obedient people. Yahweh wanted the Hebrews to see that they did not exist for the good things of this world, but rather that the good things of this world exist to help people love their God. He wanted the Hebrews to pursue a relationship with him as of primary importance. That relationship would be the source of all good and beautiful things in this world.

Without him, food, water, and peace are just idols.

But there in the shadow of Sinai, the Hebrews could not make sense of their king. They demanded the benefits of his reign without considering the knowledge or love of him their primary interest; they longed to be back under the rule of a more conventional king, like Pharaoh. Unable to make the journey back, they simply crafted an idol which represented the reign of an earthly king. Certainly, the right idol would give them a monarch who would meet more common expectations. The sin of Israel was far less extraordinary than it can sometimes appear. The golden calf was a normal feature of the Ancient Near Eastern world. Rituals performed in honor of calf idols yielded predictable results. Once the people gave the idol what it wanted, the god would grant them food, victory, and peace. The idol was simply the means to get what every ordinary person wanted.

In Moses' absence, God allowed Israel to become idolatrous, to give their hearts to the things of this world so that they would come to see the stark differences between Yahweh's people and every other people on the earth. Their treasonous idolatry was entirely conventional for its time, but it was a critical sin against the holy God. In order to instruct Moses who would need to teach the Hebrews, Yahweh told Moses that he would wipe the people out for their crimes. Meanwhile the Hebrews served the calf. They were unaware that they were on the brink of extinction; Moses stood alone between them and their holy king.

Moses, unlike the people he represented, understood that what was in jeopardy was not merely his people's lives, but the reputation of almighty Yahweh. Out of love for Moses, God relented from killing his people but, because of their sin, decided to send them away to become a normal nation in Canaan. Again, Moses understood what was really at stake in this moment. Protection, provision, national success, and victory were all meaningless without Yahweh. In other words, life for the Hebrews would not be worth living without a relationship with King Yahweh. The land, the milk, the honey, the cattle, victory in battle, and peace were all ultimately meaningless without him. Moses pleaded with Yahweh not to send them away.

In his mercy God relented and agreed to go with his people, through the desert, and into the land of promise. Neither the repentance of the Hebrews nor their goodness turned God's heart towards them. Rather Yahweh's love for Moses moved him to compassion. The Hebrews would not quickly understand God's mercy nor appreciate the role that Moses had played in saving them from God's wrath. Yet, Moses' love for God and his wisdom foreshadowed he who would be the ultimate leader of God's people.

EXODUS 33

The Lord said to Moses, "Depart; go up from here, you and the people whom you have brought up out of the land of Egypt, to the land of which I swore to Abraham, Isaac, and Jacob, saying, 'To your offspring I will give it.' I will send an angel before you, and I will drive out the Canaanites, the Amorites, the Hittites, the Perizzites, the Hivites, and the Jebusites. Go up to a land flowing with milk and honey; but I will not go up among you, lest I consume you on the way, for you are a stiff-necked people."

When the people heard this disastrous word, they mourned, and no one put on his ornaments. For the Lord had said to Moses, "Say to the people of Israel, 'You are a stiff-necked people; if for a single moment I should go up among you, I would consume you. So now take off your ornaments, that I may know what to do with you.'" Therefore, the people of Israel stripped themselves of their ornaments, from Mount Horeb onward.

Now Moses used to take the tent and pitch it outside the camp, far off from the camp, and he called it the tent of meeting. And everyone who sought the Lord would go out to the tent of meeting, which was outside the camp. Whenever Moses went out to the tent, all the people would rise up, and each would stand at his tent door, and watch Moses until he had gone into the tent. When Moses entered the tent, the pillar of cloud would descend and stand at the entrance of the tent, and the Lord would speak with Moses. And when all the people saw the pillar of cloud standing at the entrance of the tent, all the people would rise up and worship, each at his tent door. Thus, the Lord used to speak to Moses face to face, as a man speaks to his friend. When Moses turned again into the camp, his assistant Joshua the son of Nun, a young man, would not depart from the tent.

Moses said to the Lord, "See, you say to me, 'Bring up this people,' but you have not let me know whom you will send with me. Yet you have said, 'I know you by name, and you have also found favor in my sight.' Now therefore, if I have found favor in your sight, please show me now your ways, that I may know you in order to find favor in your sight. Consider too that this nation is your people." And he said, "My presence will go with you, and I will give you rest." And he said to him, "If your presence will not go with me, do not bring us up from here. For how shall it be known that I have found favor in your sight, I and your people? Is it not in your going with us, so that we are distinct, I and your people, from every other people on the face of the earth?"

And the Lord said to Moses, "This very thing that you have spoken I will do, for you have found favor in my sight, and I know you by name." Moses said, "Please show me your glory." And he said, "I will make all my goodness pass before you and will proclaim before you my name 'The Lord.' And I will be gracious to whom I will be gracious and will show mercy on whom I will show mercy. But" he said, "you cannot see my face, for man shall not see me and live." And the Lord said, "Behold, there is a place by me where you shall stand on the rock, and while my glory passes by, I will put you in a cleft of the rock, and I will cover you with my hand until I have passed by. Then I will take away my hand, and you shall see my back, but my face shall not be seen."

No Life Outside of Christ

According to Paul in Romans 1–2, all people have turned away from their true king, in part because they desire the good things of his creation but not to use as he intended. People use what he has made for satisfaction in this life rather than as so many ways to know, love, and obey the Creator. We all turn to idols, even if we did not forge them into the shape of calves. Idols promise to give us peace and prosperity, or satisfaction and purpose, without bringing us into a relationship with our God.

When we go in search of our own satisfaction, we reject our true king and so deserve his righteous wrath. But God did not abandon us to our sin. The story of Moses in Exodus 33 teaches the world that to redeem his people God sent a mediator who, out of a pure love for God, turned his back on all the joys of this world and pled for a people who, for love of this world, had turned their backs on God. God loved this mediator so deeply that he withheld his judgment and showed mercy to his people. Yahweh then will patiently abide with this mediator, who will lead his people through the rocky deserts of this life to bring them finally into his kingdom. So, Christ would ascend a wooden mountain, not only to plead for his people, but also to pay the horrible price of their treasonous sin. Moses led Israel through Sinai, while Christ leads his Church through death into Yahweh's eternal reign.

DECEMBER 10

A King Not by Earthly Standards

Since being exiled from God's good government, humanity has lived according to its own rules. Adam and Eve ate of the forbidden tree and so gained the "knowledge of good and evil." Now, rather than live by the laws of a perfectly just ruler, their descendants decide for themselves what is good and evil. Governments protect peoples by building armies. Farmers grow food by following observation, tradition, and research. By God's grace and his image in mankind, people have made incredible progress, to the point that they feel they can get by without God and his law. Human societies have in fact measured their moral rightness by their ability to succeed. Despite both small and epic failures, humanity can boast amazing successes. Roman armies created a century of peace, ancient China created the first bureaucratic state, modern societies have stopped disease, produced surplus food, and realized techno-logical advances beyond the imagination of past peoples.

The world's greatest achievements, however, only mask the fact that no human societies have every realized true, perfect, or lasting justice. All societies have suffered from inequalities, suspicion, greed, and selfishness. No matter how much economic wealth, power, or political leadership people wield, they have been unable to eliminate the moral poisons that contaminate all human relationships. Worse, regardless of their good intentions, human leaders regularly institute one kind of evil in the effort to eradicate another. Humans, it seems, tend to solve one set of problems only by creating entirely new sets of problems. It is a principle of history, that the very tools people use to fix injustices become the weapons that also war against justice.

The most effective and dangerous tool humans use—and abuse—is power. Kings and governments have always gathered strength as part of a promise to produce wealth and secure peace. Israel fell prey to the earthly temptation of power when, in 1 Samuel 8, it demanded that Samuel appoint a king for them like any other king. After Joshua's death, Israel had fallen to one power, then another. From the world's perspective, it was not difficult to see why Israel was failing. It did not have a powerful leader who could rally the people into a nation. Without a king, according to earthly standards, the Hebrews lost battles or watched foreign powers strip

them of their crops, family members, and national wealth. The
Hebrews needed an effective human government.

By earthly standards, Yahweh had not been very effective. Other
than one miraculous victory against Egypt and Joshua's successful
campaigns in Canaan, Yahweh's armies do not even appear in the
ancient legends. Other nations exerted far more power over their
neighbors. While other people groups grew into mighty nations in the
prosperous river valleys of Mesopotamia or Egypt, Yahweh's people
wandered in deserts. Yahweh was a poor king; any strong man would
have been better. It is not hard to imagine why the Hebrews, seeing
the successes of the nations around them, rejected King Yahweh.

But Israel did not realize that its problem was not Yahweh's
poor leadership. Rather, the Hebrews used flawed, spoiled earthly
standard to evaluate the omnipotent creator. Imagine if someone
used backyard kickball rules to determine that Derek Jeter, third
best hitter in all of baseball history, was a poor baseball player. One
would recognize immediately that the problem is not Derek Jeter, but
the standards. Earthly standards of kingship are pathetic, unjust, and
flawed. All societies hail rulers for having successfully wielded power
or advancing civilization. Yet the historical record clearly shows that
all of humanity's best governments have committed terrible injustices
and that all governments, at some point, collapse in failure.

Despite the failures of human governments, the Hebrews
wanted to be like every other human nation, so God granted them
a king. Saul was the man in all of Canaan most fit to function as
king. He was charismatic, strong, and volatile. He knew how to
leverage all the resources of his people to conquer their enemies.
Like any other successful human king, Saul transformed Israel
from a defeated nation into the strongest power in the region. But,
as with all other kings, his successes contained the seeds of his

failure. Saul's violence made him unstable and made Israel more vulnerable to attack. Israel did not foresee the consequences of its decision to have a normal king—in becoming like every other nation, they fell to the same fate as every other nation. Like Eve, the Hebrews believed the serpent's lie when they exchanged the holy king of heaven for an earthly king.

In truth, all human kings are failures by heavenly standards. God cannot be compared to any other government or any other king. The Hebrews demanded a leader who would give them earthly success without recognizing that all earthly success is, as the writer of Ecclesiastes argues, vanity and vapor. The success of human kings does not solve the human condition because it is only and ever a feeble shadow the eternal successes wrought by the holy king. Yahweh is the righteous God who alone can realize absolute justice by his own limitless power. All other kings are crooked imitators. Israel demanded power to succeed, but Yahweh called Israel to humility, obedience, and love. The Hebrews thought they suffered defeat from other nations because they lacked power—even though they served the omnipotent ruler of the universe. Israel could not see that its failures resulted from its refused to worship Yahweh in obedience even while it tried so desperately to succeed by the world's standards.

The Hebrews imitated every other nation in pursuing power and prosperity over justice, love, and compassion. They lusted for worldly success, which led them to idols and earthly gods. In ejecting King Yahweh, who rules over all the kings of this world, they traded eternal success for temporary gain. Israel failed to recognize that Yahweh's reign could not be measured by a world that has believed the serpent's lie and so finds knowledge of good and evil more desirable than obedience to Yahweh's commands.

PSALM 145

I will extol you, my God and King, and bless your name forever and ever. Every day I will bless you and praise your name forever and ever. Great is the Lord, and greatly to be praised, and his greatness is unsearchable.

One generation shall commend your works to another and shall declare your mighty acts. On the glorious splendor of your majesty, and on your wondrous works, I will meditate. They shall speak of the might of your awesome deeds, and I will declare your greatness.

They shall pour forth the fame of your abundant goodness and shall sing aloud of your righteousness.

The Lord is gracious and merciful, slow to anger and abounding in steadfast love. The Lord is good to all, and his mercy is over all that he has made.

All your works shall give thanks to you, O Lord, and all your saints shall bless you! They shall speak of the glory of your kingdom and tell of your power, to make known to the children of man your mighty deeds, and the glorious splendor of your kingdom. Your kingdom is an everlasting kingdom, and your dominion endures throughout all generations.

The Lord is faithful in all his words and kind in all his works.

The Lord upholds all who are falling and raises up all who are bowed down. The eyes of all look to you, and you give them their food in due season. You open your hand; you satisfy the desire of every living thing. The Lord is righteous in all his ways and kind in all his works.

The Lord is near to all who call on him, to all who call on him in truth.

He fulfills the desire of those who fear him; he also hears their cry and saves them. The Lord preserves all who love him, but all the wicked he will destroy.

My mouth will speak the praise of the Lord, and let all flesh bless his holy name forever and ever.

Jesus, King by Heaven's Standards

Those who met Jesus, and even those who followed him, measured him by common, earthly standards, and so misjudged not only him, but all other things. Israel had been waiting for the birth of a king who would be greater than all other human kings. Many political leaders had successfully established powerful earthly empires by the time of his birth: Caesar in Rome, Mithridates in Pontus, Antiochus IV over the Seleucids, even Pharaoh over the Egyptians. These kings won battles and built thriving economies. Those in Israel who waited for such a king were as angry with Jesus as they were confused. He obviously had great power but did not exercise it in a kingly way. He did not live up to earthly standards by rallying the Jews against Rome. In their frustration, his own people became deaf to his message that life is not to be measured from a flawed earthly perspective but only an eternal, heavenly perspective. Even his own followers failed to understand that Jesus was not a failure by Caesar's standards, but that Caesar was a failure by Jesus' standards. Neither the Sanhedrin nor Pontius Pilate understood that Jesus would not live down to the measure of human kings, but that through his ministry he would change the definition of kingship forever.

By heavenly standards, Jesus is the only king. He brings his infinite power to the lost and the dying, the sick and the sinners. Through what the world can only define as weakness, Jesus exercised unthinkable power to save his people. By enduring the most humiliating death at the hands of a corrupt government, he most gloriously defeated death—which no governments will ever be able to conquer, no matter what promises they may make.

THE KING

God is the King. While Christians have many ways of understanding this phrase, it expresses, at its heart, a truth—God is a
political being. The entire picture of the creation is of a paradise
rightly ordered by God's rule. His spoken laws weave the material
universe together into a place of goodness and love. These two
things are not coincidental but rather causal. God's kingly rule is
the source of everything that is right, happy, and good.

In the fall, Satan counters God's kingship with a false promise. He
lies to Eve by telling her that when she rejects God's rule, she will be
free to govern herself. Sin is, by its very nature, a political decision to
exchange the Creator's law for anyone else's. In fact, according to the
Bible there are only two choices: be a subject of Satan's government
or of God's, a slave to death or a slave to life. This is the heart of the
debate between Satan and Jesus Christ during his temptation. He
faces the same dreadful decision that Eve faced. Satan offered him
food and peace should he only choose to reject God's kingship.

After Genesis 3, the Scriptures tell the story of how humans attempted to govern the world not as emissaries of the Creator's kingly rule but according to their own desires. The disaster that ensued was beyond comparison in either the ancient or modern worlds. Humans became so evil that God decided to expunge all humanity except the one person, and his family, who continued to make God his king. Noah's act of faith flowed out of a unique commitment to Yahweh's rule. It is hard to imagine the pressure he faced to follow his own desires, to do as the entire world was doing at the time. But Noah obeyed and was saved; the world committed treason and was judged. Then history took a different course. In Genesis 9, God decided to set humanity on a new path so that it might avoid the unspeakable evil of the years before the flood. He created an institution to imitate his own rule; he gave humanity government.

Blessed with this new tool, human beings now unleashed the creativity that comes with cooperation under authority. Two chapters later they built the greatest human society, possibly in all of history. The tower and surrounding city under the rule of Nimrod was so great that it had the potential reach even the heavens—that is, the perfection of human paradise. The good of this government, however, did not follow from God's rule but from humanity's rule. In the second act of judgment since the fall, God scattered the citizens of the great tower and forced them into smaller societies. Made in his image, humanity found that government possesses incredible power.

Against the temptation to rebuild the great tower on this earth, one felt by all, God constructed against a very different building under a very different government. Through the call of Abraham, God began to restore his kingship over the world. He carefully designed a vehicle by which he would reassert his rule—the nation.

God promised he would create, through Abraham, a people as numerous as the sands of the seashore. From Isaac he brought by miracle the children who would become the nation of Israel. Thus, the Scriptures sets ever increasing levels of bureaucracy as milestones that mark the progress of God's redeeming plan: Abraham to Joseph, Joseph to Moses, and Joshua to David. These levels of government represent the slow but sure return of the Almighty King. As they set the historic patterns and prophetic pictures of what his return would look like. God fights for Israel at the Red Sea and then against the Hittites, Jebusites, and Amalekites. He sends bread and brings water out of the rocks to sustain his people. He dictates a royal decree that becomes Israel's law as the divine legislator. Should Israel have obeyed its king, they would have experienced the benefits of a perfect government-fruitfulness, plenty, and peace of a kind only equaled by Eden's paradise.

But Israel rejected her king. The Scriptures reveal in painful detail how Israel turned from its king at the edge of the promised land, in the long march through the desert, and even while living in his land as his subjects. Yahweh told Samuel clearly that by asking for their own king the people had finally rejected Yahweh as their king. Their treason seemed to be absolute, and so Israel was doomed. The people of Israel would now fall to ruin not necessarily by God's judgment but because every king other than Yahweh fails and brings the people with him. Under Saul Israel suffered injustices and faced war, but when times grew darkest, God promised to save his people by anointing a new king. He did not choose a king who ruled by his own word, but a king who loved God's heart. David came to the throne to bring Israel back under King Yahweh. Under David Israel found peace and prosperity, by the enduring grace and love of God which established a government obedient to him. David was a king under a King. It was for this season that Israel felt the glory of living under God's rule.

God's redemption is, by its very nature, a political act by which the Monarch of all Creation destroys all other claims to authority and returns to his rightful place as Ruler of all. Israel made the mistake of thinking that David and his heirs were the kings that would make their nation great and so turned away from God's laws. The writings of Moses should have been clear enough—every other rule leads to ruin. Under human rulers Israel, like any nation in the history of the world, would suffer devastating defeats until its people became nothing more than a remnant in a foreign land. It is from this, the lowest point in Israel's life and perhaps the darkest moment in human history, that God uttered a promise: David was only precursor of who was to come. Redemption will only be realized for humanity when the son of David sits on David's throne. This king will rule for eternity. He will pull all other rulers under his feet. He will destroy all his enemies; he will redeem all the nations of the world by his love. All that is good and right will only be established when God is once again the king of all creation and humanity finally bows the knee to its one, true, and rightful Sovereign.

DECEMBER 11

The Beauty of Sacrifices

The Almighty King of creation defeated Pharaoh and the Egyptian gods and led his people out of Egypt. Yahweh exerted his royal prerogative over the water, weather, and even the firstborn children of that mighty nation. While other kings had to rely on armies staffed by their own people, Yahweh defended his people with pillars of fire, then floods of water. The Hebrews became a nation under their true king who cared for his people's needs as he led them across the deserts of Sinai to the land that he would establish as his capital. He rained bread, supplied quail, and provided water. Then, as the Hebrews waited at the base of Mount Sinai, Yahweh delivered the law that would make the wandering people a nation. He then promised that under his law the land to which they were traveling would become a second Eden.

But the Hebrews rejected their king and, by consequence, their identity as his people. When Aaron formed the golden calf and the Hebrews swore loyalty to it, their crime was chiefly political. By giving their loyalty to another god, the Hebrews rejected Yahweh as their king. Today those in the Modern West define worshipping a god as a purely religious practice. But during Moses' time, loyalty to a god was a political decision. Gods commanded governments over people in a particular land. By turning to a local deity in the form of a golden calf, the Hebrews were simply following the political common sense of their day but doing so was also treason against Yahweh. The Israelites' crime was worthy of the most extreme punishment; their treason was a cosmic crime.

The Hebrews' treachery, however, was more than political; it was a moral crime as well. Yahweh is not just a king; he is also holy and therefore the only source of all moral goodness. To oppose Yahweh is to do evil. For any other people, changing gods would come with moving to a new place. But Yahweh is not another god— he is righteousness in himself. Isaiah fell to the ground in terror before Yahweh's moral perfection (Isaiah 6:5); Moses himself would have died in the presence of Yahweh's perfection had he not been hidden in the cleft of a rock (Exodus 33:29). The Hebrews did not yet understand that by rejecting Yahweh, they had become corrupt and subject to his righteous wrath. So that he might continue to lead his sinful people, God needed to erect something that would stand between Yahweh and his people. This new thing would not keep Israel away from God but would rather keep them safe from the holy God.

God alerted Moses that he would no longer tolerate the Hebrews because of their sin, but Moses intervened. According to the Scriptures, Yahweh responded to Moses' plea by relenting and agreeing to remain the king of Israel (Exodus 33). He would continue to travel with his people so that one day he might live permanently with them. In his frustration over the Hebrews' sin, Moses broke the original stone tablet containing the Ten Commandments, the Law of Yahweh for Israel. After Moses returned to Mount Sinai, God again chiseled the Ten Commandments into tablets, but in addition to the moral law, Yahweh created a priestly system that would allow his people to remain alive as he lived with them.

At the center of this new system was a place of meeting which Yahweh would visit to lead and guide his people. This mobile seat was called a tent of meeting, which God commanded to be built out into a tabernacle that could be moved as Israel moved. The heart of both the tent and the tabernacle was a place made holy so that it could be Yahweh's chamber, at the center of which was an ark that would become Yahweh's seat. God then protected Israel by surrounding this holy chamber with ceremonies, practices, and rules that became a buffer between he and his people. In addition, Moses instituted rituals that would prepare the priests who could tend to the holy space. But the priests were not in themselves able to become pure enough to enter the holy space. Worse, the Hebrews could not be made holy enough even to have Yahweh in their camp. To ensure the safety of the priests and the people, Yahweh provided a detailed system of sacrifices.

In the Ancient Near East, sacrifices to gods were meals prepared by people to meet the appetite of their local god. Yahweh gave Israel a revolutionary new sacrificial system. In these sacrifices, Israel's priests would symbolically take out the penalty of the people's sins against Yahweh on animals so that he would not consume the people by his holiness. Sacrifices did not feed God; God, in his great mercy, gave sacrifices to Israel so that they might remain close to him. The system that Yahweh put in place through the extended law system reflected the sacrifices that the Hebrews made during the night of the Passover, when God brought them away from the Egyptians. In that miraculous night, Yahweh commanded his angel to bring judgment against evil, but to bypass any house that had the lamb's blood upon the lintel. In this way, Yahweh taught the people of Israel how they would relate to their king. As with Adam and Eve after the fall, death would be the only way for people to live with Yahweh.

LEVITICUS 4:1–12, 22–31

And the Lord spoke to Moses, saying, "Speak to the people of Israel, saying, If anyone sins unintentionally in any of the Lord's commandments about things not to be done, and does any one of them, if it is the anointed priest who sins, thus bringing guilt on the people, then he shall offer for the sin that he has committed a bull from the herd without blemish to the Lord for a sin offering. He shall bring the bull to the entrance of the tent of meeting before the Lord and lay his hand on the head of the bull and kill the bull before the Lord. And the anointed priest shall take some of the blood of the bull and bring it into the tent of meeting, and the priest shall dip his finger in the blood and sprinkle part of the blood seven times before the Lord in front of the veil of the sanctuary. And the priest shall put some of the blood on the horns of the altar of fragrant incense before the Lord that is in the tent of meeting, and all the rest of the blood of the bull he shall pour out at the base of the altar of burnt offering that is at the entrance of the tent of meeting. And all the fat of the bull of the sin offering he shall remove from it, the fat that covers the entrails and all the fat that is on the entrails and the two kidneys with the fat that is on them at the loins and the long lobe of the liver that he shall remove with the kidneys (just as these are taken from the ox of the sacrifice of the peace offerings); and the priest shall burn them on the altar of burnt offering. But the skin of the bull and all its flesh, with its head, its legs, its entrails, and its dung—all the rest of the bull—he shall carry outside the camp to a clean place, to the ash heap, and shall burn it up on a fire of wood. On the ash heap it shall be burned up. . . ..

"When a leader sins, doing unintentionally any one of all the things that by the commandments of the Lord his God ought not to be done, and realizes his guilt, or the sin which he has committed is made known to him, he shall bring as his offering a goat, a male without blemish, and shall lay his hand on the head of the goat and kill it in the place where they kill the burnt offering before the Lord; it is a sin offering. Then the priest shall take some of the blood of the sin offering with his finger and put it on the horns of the altar of burnt offering and pour out the rest of its blood at the base of the altar of burnt offering. And all its fat he shall burn on the altar, like the fat of the sacrifice of peace offerings. So, the priest shall make atonement for him for his sin, and he shall be forgiven.

"If anyone of the common people sins unintentionally in doing any one of the things that by the Lord's commandments ought not to be done, and realizes his guilt, or the sin which he has committed is made known to him, he shall bring for his offering a goat, a female without blemish, for his sin which he has committed. And he shall lay his hand on the head of the sin offering and kill the sin offering in the place of burnt offering. And the priest shall take some of its blood with his finger and put it on the horns of the altar of burnt offering and pour out all the rest of its blood at the base of the altar. And all its fat he shall remove, as the fat is removed from the peace offerings, and the priest shall burn it on the altar for a pleasing aroma to the Lord. And the priest shall make atonement for him, and he shall be forgiven.

Jesus, the Once-for-All Sacrifice

The religious and political life of Israel was a complex culture of rituals and ceremonies built around a system of sacrifices which culminated in atonement. In the atonement, a priest would place his hands on a perfect lamb without blemish to transfer Israel's sins to the lamb, and then kill it. Through this sacrifice, Yahweh taught Israel the depth of their sin against him. Only something pure could take upon itself the death the Hebrews deserved. In the second part of the ceremony, the priest would again place his hands on an animal, this time a goat, then send the goat out of the encampment to bear the people's sins outside the camp, where it would die from exposure or wild animals. At its most fundamental level, this sacrificial system protected Israel from God's holiness. At another level, the system taught the Hebrews the most important lesson about their relationship to Yahweh, a lesson that they would only finally learn when the one who was the perfect lamb and effective scapegoat appeared. The sheep and goats of Jewish sacrifices were God's provisional plan to protect Israel for a time, but they could never pay the debt owed by those who committed cosmic treason against the holy Yahweh. Only one of infinite perfection could take upon himself sins against the perfect God. Thus Jesus, the sinless son of God, became our Passover lamb, the one about whom all of God's laws, ceremonies, sacrifices, and celebrations spoke.

DECEMBER 12

The Example of Redemption

The road from Sinai to Canaan was long and difficult. Israel grew weary of its exile from the Egypt and longed to be back on the banks of the Nile. Facing the long road through a wilderness, the people succumbed to fear and temptation. They routinely rejected God's kingship by disobeying Moses, his chosen vice-regent. Despite their stubborn rebelliousness, God provided for his people and defeated their enemies. But the process of becoming the people of Yahweh was not over. After forty years of wandering the Hebrews then had to fight a military campaign against an entrenched enemy. Under the leadership of Joshua, God would make the land of Canaan a renewed Eden which meant that the land must be made holy. All the people in Yahweh's land would need to obey him as king and no other. But King Yahweh was unusual to a people used to worldly kings.

In the Ancient Near East, kings were not merely strong leaders with militaries, they were servants of their gods. The gods were the true inhabitants of the natural world; their actions and decisions determined natural events. Human beings learned to live in the wake of the gods' lives. Priests and political leaders read the signs and collected the data. They knew how to predict the rains and what to do to win in battles. Serving the gods was the science of daily life. Kings themselves functioned as the people's chief representative to the gods whose service ensured the people's success. The Canaanites served Ba'al, one of the most influential and powerful gods of Mesopotamia. The character of his leadership among the desert climate of that region was well-known and well-respected. The Amorites honored Amurru and his wife, Asra-tum (Asherah), for crops and fertility. Canaanite and Amorite kings led the people in their routine service of these gods, daily serving their idols food and performing rituals.

For those who lived in the ancient world, honoring the gods seemed like common sense. The greatest scholars of the day were required to attend school for nearly a decade so that they could learn to read the signs necessary to predict the gods. Established cities contained libraries of exact and well-researched texts. For the Hebrews, the temptation to serve the gods of the age was not outlandish or exotic, but rather fed into the Israelites' tendency to live the same way as every other culture.

But God was not like the other gods. The gods demanded service to appease their own appetites. Yahweh ruled his people for their security and flourishing. The gods were elements of the nat-ural world whose actions determined all the events of the physical universe. Yahweh was holy; he was the only true God who created the universe and so was above it and beyond it. Service to the gods was the essence of political strife between peoples. Yahweh was the King of all peoples whose rule alone could unify the world. Yahweh was unlike any of the gods, strange to all peoples, which made serving him strange in the Ancient Near East.

Compared to other Ancient Near Eastern societies, the Hebrews were strange. While other peoples were used by the gods as farmers and fighters, Yahweh fought for his people so that they might flourish under his reign. Life for the Hebrews was not to be a calculated interaction with the gods but rather a commitment of humble obedience to the Creator who loved and protected them. As the Hebrews entered the promised land, God made clear to Israel its purpose in the world: to abandon the common science of the day, avoid the tendency to predict the natural world by divination, and resist the pull of belonging to the other peoples around them. From the call of Abraham through the miraculous Exodus from Egypt, God had separated the Hebrews from all the peoples of the world so that they might set an example of redemption. They would show that the world that it was as it ought to be but was fallen and alienated from its Creator. Through obedience to the one true holy God, the Hebrews would mark out the way of new creation.

To prepare them for their redemptive work in the promised land God gave the Hebrews stern warnings. Should they turn back from their responsibilities, God would exile them from the new Eden as a powerful reminder of humanity's original fall. He was clear that failure would not result from miscalculations about the god's wills, but rather from failing to obey his perfect law which God had graciously written and preserved.

When Israel had conquered the land, Joshua gave its people an ultimatum: serve Yahweh or reject Yahweh. This radical statement proved the strangeness of the Hebrew people. Nations in that time chose a god, and usually a goddess, to honor while practicing deference to the other gods as well. God's people would become aliens to their world if they confessed that no gods were equal to him. While other people served their gods if they enjoyed success, the people of God were to obey him even if doing so meant suffering a long exile through desert wildernesses or slavery to foreign governments. Yahweh is real, though the world thinks he is fiction. Yahweh is the only truth, though the world believes lies.

From the murder of Abel to the death of Joshua, God had reversed humanity's exile. No more would people wander through the thistles of a lawless world. Canaan was the land of plenty and peace under God's reign. His people had not freed themselves from their enemies—God had done everything for them. All he required was obedience to his laws and trust in his promises. But in this world such things are too strange, in the same way that for sinners' true obedience to God is impossible. To bring people back under his kingly rule, God himself would need to restore their hearts.

JOSHUA 24:14-28

Now therefore fear the Lord and serve him in sincerity and in faithfulness. Put away the gods that your fathers served beyond the river and in Egypt and serve the Lord. And if it is evil in your eyes to serve the Lord, choose this day whom you will serve, whether the gods your fathers served in the region beyond the river, or the gods of the Amorites in whose land you dwell. But as for me and my house, we will serve the Lord."

Then the people answered, "Far be it from us that we should forsake the Lord to serve other gods, for it is the Lord our God who brought us and our fathers up from the land of Egypt, out of the house of slavery, and who did those great signs in our sight and preserved us in all the way that we went, and among all the peoples through whom we passed. And the Lord drove out before us all the peoples, the Amorites who lived in the land. Therefore, we also will serve the Lord, for he is our God."

But Joshua said to the people, "You are not able to serve the Lord, for he is a holy God. He is a jealous God; he will not forgive your transgressions or your sins. If you forsake the Lord and serve foreign gods, then he will turn and do you harm and consume you, after having done you good." And the people said to Joshua, "No, but we will serve the Lord." Then Joshua said to the people, "You are witnesses against yourselves that you have chosen the Lord, to serve him." And they said, "We are witnesses." He said, "Then put away the foreign gods that are among you, and incline your heart to the Lord, the God of Israel." And the people said to Joshua, "The Lord our God we will serve, and his voice we will obey." So, Joshua made a covenant with the people that day, and put in place statutes and rules for them at Shechem. And Joshua wrote these words in the Book of the Law of God. And he took a large stone and set it up there under the terebinth that was by the sanctuary of the Lord. And Joshua said to all the people, "Behold, this stone shall be a witness against us, for it has heard all the words of the Lord that he spoke to us. Therefore, it shall be a witness against you, lest you deal falsely with your God." So, Joshua sent the people away, every man to his inheritance.

A People Redeemed

God cleared the twisted bramble of the fallen world to recreate the original garden in the land of Canaan. The renewed garden was the home of his presence in the tabernacle, from which his laws emanated. According to the Scriptures, the world of the gods was a lie, but the Word of God is reality. Obedience to his kingly reign is life in a world of death. But Israel, unable to keep that law, followed Adam and Eve's deadly pattern. The flaw of redemption cannot be found in the history of God's kingship but in humanity's stubborn refusal to obey it. Even though humanity continuously rejects Yahweh's kingship and despises is promise of redemption, Yahweh pursues humanity still. Rather than abandon it to self-imposed exile from its Creator, God came to earth as a man who would obey his law to save mankind. Jesus Christ is humanity as humanity was created to be—the perfect son of Yahweh. We now belong to God through his obedience as we trust in him and him alone to restore us and the universe.

DECEMBER 13

Kinsman Redeemer

A famine during the time of the judges forced Elimelech to go into exile in Moab with his wife and two sons. He took his family away from the home in which he had grown from a son into a father. Moab a neighboring land located to the east of Israel, across the Jordan. While Moabites were descendants of Lot and therefore racial relatives of the Hebrews, they were also gentile pagans who built their society around the worship of Chemosh. Every routine activity was informed by service to this god. In the ancient world, the deity of a people not only defined their values and their practices, but also informed their identities. Chemosh was the Moabite version of Ba'al, who was the Canaanite god of war and fertility.

For Elimelech to live by Yahweh's laws in the land of Chemosh meant that his family would be foreigners in a foreign land. He and his family would appear odd for living as cultural outcasts. Times must have been desperate for Elimelech to make his live as aliens in another land. As difficult as it must have been for Hebrews to live in Moab, the death of Elimelech must have plunged his wife, Naomi, into severe hardship. She would now have to rely on her two sons for survival. In that day, a woman's standing came from her husband or male children, thus the death of Naomi's two sons must have been nothing less than a total tragedy. Without husband or sons, Naomi was destitute—a social pariah who threatened the reputation of anyone with whom she interacted. Naomi had been a political exile; now she was a social exile. She was without hope or possibility. Her terrible situation was made even more dire by the fact that she now had to care for her two widowed daughters-in-law.

Naomi decided to go back to her people and eke out the rest of her life on her husband's property, which she did not have legal right to own. To save her daughters-in-law the indignity of another layer of exile, she counseled them to stay in their homeland. Ruth refused. The dedication of Ruth is difficult to explain, since by remaining with Naomi, Ruth was consigning herself to a lifetime of alienation. According to rabbinic traditions, Ruth was also the daughter of the Moabite king, which meant that she left the protection and dignity of life in a royal family to support a destitute widow who possessed no status. By making Naomi's people her people and Naomi's God her God, Ruth would be reducing her life to caring for a social outcast as a penniless exile.

Naomi had left Canaan as a woman of standing but now crossed the Jordan River destitute. She would endure a uniquely painful exile—she would live as a foreigner in her own land, a stranger to her own people. Her only hope for survival came from the Mosaic law, which required farmers to leave the corners of their fields unharvested so that the helplessly poor could glean scraps enough to live. To increase her chances, Naomi settled on the border of Boaz's farm, a wealthy man who obeyed the Mosaic law with a pronounced generosity.

Boaz was wealthy and kind—one whose station in life depended on his public reputation. But Boaz was also more.

According to Levitical law, a man could marry his brother's widow and thereby redeem her. This redemption was a thorough and complete transformation of a woman's social standing from exiled outcast to a woman of respect and stature. While redemption was an absolute reversal of fortunes for the widow, it was costly to the redeemer. He had to purchase the widow's land and debts, and, in some cases, take on the indignity of his brother's reputation. The cost of redeeming Naomi was particularly high. Not only would a relative have to purchase Elimelech's land, but he would also have to marry a Moabite, which could ruin his standing in Hebrew society. The social stigma of marrying a gentile made the cost of redeeming Naomi steep—for some, it was insurmountable. When Ruth came to Boaz in the night, she uncovered his feet to show him that he was, by Mosaic law, a kinsman who could redeem Naomi. But Boaz was second in line for this responsibility. He could have simply ignored Ruth and told her to find Elimelech's brother, but he did not.

In keeping with the law, Boaz met Elimelech's brother in front of the city elders. Boaz alerted this man of standing to his responsibility to redeem Elimelech's wife, but the man refused. The biblical text does not state the reasons for the man's refusal, but those reasons are too obvious to have to list. To redeem Naomi was to irrevocably damage the man's own standing and position. Redeeming the widow by marrying her gentile daughter-in-law was a cost too great for Elimelech's brother to bear—but not for Boaz. Boaz did not count the cost to his reputation when he reached down to a broken, impoverished, social outcast. He spent significant money and his valuable reputation to restore Naomi so that he might end her deep exile. The text tells us that this sacrificial act was not only a picture of God's unimaginable love for his people, but also the very act that would lead to the birth of David, the king whose line of children would include Jesus Christ himself.

RUTH 4:1-12

Now Boaz had gone up to the gate and sat down there. And behold, the redeemer, of whom Boaz had spoken, came by. So Boaz said, "Turn aside, friend; sit down here." And he turned aside and sat down. And he took ten men of the elders of the city and said, "Sit down here." So, they sat down. Then he said to the redeemer, "Naomi, who has come back from the country of Moab, is selling the parcel of land that belonged to our relative Elimelech. So, I thought I would tell you of it and say, 'Buy it in the presence of those sitting here and in the presence of the elders of my people.' If you will redeem it, redeem it. But if you will not, tell me, that I may know, for there is no one besides you to redeem it, and I come after you." And he said, "I will redeem it." Then Boaz said, "The day you buy the field from the hand of Naomi, you also acquire Ruth the Moabite, the widow of the dead, in order to perpetuate the name of the dead in his inheritance." Then the redeemer said, "I cannot redeem it for myself, lest I impair my own inheritance. Take my right of redemption yourself, for I cannot redeem it."

Now this was the custom in former times in Israel concerning redeeming and exchanging: to confirm a transaction, the one drew off his sandal and gave it to the other, and this was the manner of attesting in Israel. So when the redeemer said to Boaz, "Buy it for yourself," he drew off his sandal. Then Boaz said to the elders and all the people, "You are witnesses this day that I have bought from the hand of Naomi all that belonged to Elimelech and all that belonged to Chilion and to Mahlon. Also, Ruth the Moabite, the widow of Mahlon, I have bought to be my wife, to perpetuate the name of the dead in his inheritance, that the name of the dead may not be cut off from among his brothers and from the gate of his native place. You are witnesses this day." Then all the people who were at the gate and the elders said, "We are witnesses. May the Lord make the woman, who is coming into your house, like Rachel and Leah, who together built up the house of Israel. May you act worthily in Ephrathah and be renowned in Bethlehem, and may your house be like the house of Perez, whom Tamar bore to Judah, because of the offspring that the Lord will give you by this young woman."

Redeemed by God Himself

We are unable to calculate the indignity that God bore by taking on human flesh and living among a sinful people. Whether we realize it or not, we are a people in deep exile who live outside the righteous government of our Creator King. We are slaves to sin and servants of death. Like a widow in the ancient world with a gentile widowed daughter-in-law, we are without hope and without possibility. Like Elimelech's brother, God has given the powers of this world the chance to redeem our brokenness, but they have neither the wherewithal nor the righteousness to do so. Instead, our elder brother abandoned his status of unimaginable glory to take on our shame that we might be restored. Out of the union of this historic condescension came the one who would redeem his people from the power of death by taking on their sin to restore them to the dignity of being called the children of the most High God.

DECEMBER 14

Yahweh's King

Since Adam and Eve first planted crops in a world twisted with thorns and thistles, human beings have lived in a world without their God. The disorder of the external world has been a physical extension of the human heart's sinful rebellion. In his mercy, God granted humanity governments to limit the social evil that spills out from corrupt human hearts. After the flood, nearly every group of human beings constructed a cultural system with a king at its head. Israel left Egypt in the miraculous Exodus and entered Ancient Mesopotamia, a world of gods and kings.

During the time of David, the world was defined by the lives of gods—lives that played out in natural events. By the will of the gods, dry seasons led to poor harvests and victory in battle led to increased wealth. However, the reason for these events were complicated by the fact that the gods lived their lives beyond human sight and hearing. To manage the people of their land, the gods chose kings to serve them and obey their will. If a king interacted properly with the gods, the kingdom he ruled would thrive. But if he failed, the results were disastrous for the people. The heightened role of the king meant that the choice of king fell to the gods. Kings became superhuman beings; their reign became the touchstone of the people's survival.

From the defeat of Pharaoh to the consecration of David, Yahweh recreated the idea of kingship, for he claimed not to be the master of a particular province but the only God over all the earth. Yahweh did not need a human king to secure his estate while he

labored in unseen realms. Rather, through the plagues and the miracles of the Exodus, it was clear that Yahweh ruled over all places. He
was the only God and so his king would not rule a lower kingdom in
service to an unknown realm. Yahweh's king would be a leader who
prepared the earth for Yahweh's reign—the earth was not a side-
show; it was the object of Yahweh's loving rule. Unlike other kings,
who were required to make risky interpretations of natural events to
understand the gods' wills, Yahweh ensured that Moses had written
his law down for the king and the people to follow.

One of the most revolutionary aspects of Israel's king was that
he was not tasked with serving Yahweh's appetites. Instead, Yahweh
appointed a king to feed, protect, and restore his people so that
the reign of David actually reversed the ancient view of kingship.
Rather than represent the people to a murky higher realm, David
was tasked with ensuring that the kingdom of Israel became the
permanent home and arena of Yahweh's direct, clear, and just rule.
In biblical language, Yahweh established a nation and a king to
serve as the apparatus by which he would restore his relationship
with all peoples on all the earth. While every other king of the day
worked to secure control of his god's feudal holdings, Israel's king
would build Yahweh a home to which every tribe could come.

But the Hebrews grew enamored by the cultures around them
and demanded a king like other nations, by consequence they
demanded a god like other nations. Unfortunately, Israel's first king,
Saul, lived down to Israel's expectations as he sought the knowledge of heavenly realms to secure victories. He treated God's laws
like any Ancient Near Eastern king, but Yahweh was no Ancient
Near Eastern god. The failure of Saul's leadership became evident
when he could not divine a way around or through Goliath. It was
David's love for Yahweh that revealed to Israel how its king must

differ from those of other nations.

David was a man after God's own heart. He understood that Israel's fortunes were determined by Yahweh's grace and measured by Israel's love for Yahweh. Yet at times David slipped back into the ways of the world. To advantage his own kingly prerogative, he disobeyed God's laws when he took Bathsheba to himself. Rather than trust that God would protect Israel, he decided to number his own people as a way of securing protection. David was not a superhuman king, but a flawed person who all too easily reverted back to the world's ways. In the end his failures disqualified him from being what Israel's king should have been—the one to build a home for Yahweh. But, he knew, as did Moses, that this home would be the very life of Israel and the great redemption of the world.

2 SAMUEL 7

Now when the king lived in his house and the Lord had given him rest from all his surrounding enemies, the king said to Nathan the prophet, "See now, I dwell in a house of cedar, but the ark of God dwells in a tent." And Nathan said to the king, "Go, do all that is in your heart, for the Lord is with you."

But that same night the word of the Lord came to Nathan, "Go and tell my servant David, 'Thus says the Lord: Would you build me a house to dwell in? I have not lived in a house since the day I brought up the people of Israel from Egypt to this day, but I have been moving about in a tent for my dwelling. In all places where I have moved with all the people of Israel, did I speak a word with any of the judges of Israel, whom I commanded to shepherd my people Israel, saying, "Why have you not built me a house of cedar?"' Now, therefore, thus you shall say to my servant David, 'Thus says the Lord of hosts, I took you from the pasture, from following the sheep, that you should be prince over my people Israel. And I have been with you wherever you went and have cut off all your enemies from before you. And I will make for you a great name, like the name of the great ones of the earth. And I will appoint a place for my people Israel and will plant them, so that they may dwell in their own place and be disturbed no more. And violent men shall afflict them no more, as formerly, from the time that I appointed judges over my people Israel. And I will give you rest from all your enemies. Moreover, the Lord declares to you that the Lord will make you a house. When your days are fulfilled and you lie down with your fathers, I will raise up your offspring after you, who shall come from your body, and I will establish his kingdom. He shall build a house for my name, and I will establish the throne of his kingdom forever. I will be to him a father, and he shall be to me a son. When he commits iniquity, I will discipline him with the rod of men, with the stripes of the sons of men, but my steadfast love will not depart from him, as I took it from Saul, whom I put away from before you. And your house and your kingdom shall be made sure forever before me. Your throne shall be established forever.'" In accordance with all these words, and in accordance with all this vision, Nathan spoke to David.

Then King David went in and sat before the Lord and said, "Who am I, O Lord God, and what is my house, that you have brought me thus far? And yet this was a small thing in your eyes, O Lord God. You have spoken also of your servant's house for a great while to come, and this is instruction for mankind, O Lord God! And what more can David say to you? For you know your servant, O Lord God! Because of your promise, and according to your own heart, you have brought about all this greatness, to make your servant know it. Therefore you are great, O Lord God. For there is none like you, and there is no God besides you, according to all that we have heard with our ears. And who is like your people Israel, the one nation on earth whom God went to redeem to be his people, making himself a name and doing for them great and awesome things by driving out before your people, whom you redeemed for yourself from Egypt, a nation, and its gods? And you established for yourself your people Israel to be your people forever. And you, O Lord, became their God. And now, O Lord God, confirm forever the word that you have spoken concerning your servant and concerning his house, and do as you have spoken. And your name will be magnified forever, saying, 'The Lord of hosts is God over Israel,' and the house of your servant David will be established before you. For you, O Lord of hosts, the God of Israel, have made this revelation to your servant, saying, 'I will build you a house.' Therefore your servant has found courage to pray this prayer to you. And now, O Lord God, you are God, and your words are true, and you have promised this good thing to your servant. Now therefore may it please you to bless the house of your servant, so that it may continue forever before you. For you, O Lord God, have spoken, and with your blessing shall the house of your servant be blessed forever."

Yahweh's Perfect King

All the kings of Israel failed. After David, Solomon began his reign in loving obedience to Yahweh. God blessed him with the responsibility of completing the job for which God created kingship—to build a permanent home for Yahweh. And yet Solomon, like his father, turned back to the ways of the world; after him only a few kings understood who they were supposed to be or who their God was. In the wreckage created by Israel's kings, God sent prophets to speak of a king who would come in the line of David and restore the glory of Israel. But all too easily Jewish leaders let their hopes be defined by the ambitions of this world. They yearned for the political intelligence that might help them secure victories, rather than obedience that grows out of a love for Yahweh above all things.

Harboring ambitions for political success in their hearts, Israel's leaders became blind to their true king which the Holy Spirit had promised. Against the model of the world's mighty rulers, Jesus Christ was born to a poor, unmarried couple in a small, impoverished town. Unlike all other rulers who lay claim to power, he was the light of men, God himself who would tabernacle with his people. While the Jews would cling tightly to the temple, they missed the one for whom the temple was built. Jesus was not merely a leader or a servant of the nation, he was and is the permanent presence of Yahweh for his people in all places and in all times, over all the earth. Through Jesus alone Yahweh will redeem all things back to himself.

DECEMBER 15

The Nation of Yahweh

The Hebrews had a robust understanding of gods and how they worked. But Yahweh was unlike any other god.

Other gods made demands of their people, sometimes in ceremonies or in acts of war or trade. Yahweh, on the other hand, entered a covenant with a single people through which he promised to love and bless them. Political relationships in that day often happened when a lord, or superior nation, entered a covenant with a lesser power, or vassal nation. Yahweh's covenant relationship with Israel fit the standard pattern. However, in an unusual decision, Yahweh entered a one-sided covenant with his people. While Abraham slept, Yahweh walked through torn animal pieces to represent to Abraham's descendants that he alone would fulfill all the promises to the Hebrews. In this way God made it clear that despite Israel's failures, the Lord would fulfill his promises to Israel, promises to bless the world through Abraham's seed.

Other nations existed for the benefit of the gods they served. Gods used nations for their own ends. But Yahweh exhibited a new characteristic: faithfulness. He kept his promises for the sake of his people and for the sake of the world, even though his vassal nation did not keep its promises. Yahweh's relationship with Israel was defined by love.

The covenant God entered with Abraham and with Abraham's descendants was very specific. He would bless Abraham's seed with a king who would serve as the chief agent in building for Yahweh a home among his people. Although Abraham and his children committed themselves to the covenant relationship with Yahweh, they each failed in their turn—from Isaac's machinations and Jacob's lies to the Hebrews' faithlessness in Egypt. Moses himself disobeyed God, as did Israel's first king, Saul. Had Yahweh entered a standard covenant with Israel, he would have had every right to destroy the nation and begin again with another people. But he did not hinge his covenant on Israel's commitment; he anchored his relationship with Israel in his own faithfulness.

After he secured the promised land for his people, Yahweh provided leaders called judges to help Israel stay true to its covenant. Both Israel and the judges failed miserably, despite a few moments during which Israel returned to its covenant with Yahweh. Finally, Israel shattered its relationship with God when its people rejected Yahweh in an effort to secure a king like every other nation. God then gave Israel the best human king, but Saul brought ruin on Israel. It was at this moment that God raised up the person whom he had promised for Israel. David would be the king who would lead the people back to the Lord and prepare Israel to receive the Lord. Again, the will of man failed. David disqualified himself from building Yahweh a permanent home when he sinned with Bathsheba.

By every measure, God should have abandoned his commitments to Israel. Yet despite every faithless deed, God raised up a man under whose leadership he would finally realize his great promises to his disobedient people—Solomon would build Yahweh a house. That house would not only be the fulfillment of his promises, but it would also represent Yahweh's enduring love. It would stand as a monument to his forgiveness.

1 KINGS 8:22-61

Then Solomon stood before the altar of the Lord in the presence of all the assembly of Israel and spread out his hands toward heaven, and said, "O Lord, God of Israel, there is no God like you, in heaven above or on earth beneath, keeping covenant and showing steadfast love to your servants who walk before you with all their heart; you have kept with your servant David my father what you declared to him. You spoke with your mouth, and with your hand have fulfilled it this day. Now therefore, O Lord, God of Israel, keep for your servant David my father what you have promised him, saying, 'You shall not lack a man to sit before me on the throne of Israel, if only your sons pay close attention to their way, to walk before me as you have walked before me.' Now therefore, O God of Israel, let your word be confirmed, which you have spoken to your servant David my father.

"But will God indeed dwell on the earth? Behold, heaven and the highest heaven cannot contain you; how much less this house that I have built! Yet have regard to the prayer of your servant and to his plea, O Lord my God, listening to the cry and to the prayer that your servant prays before you this day, that your eyes may be open night and day toward this house, the place of which you have said, 'My name shall be there,' that you may listen to the prayer that your servant offers toward this place. And listen to the plea of your servant and of your people Israel when they pray toward this place. And listen in heaven your dwelling place, and when you hear, forgive.

"If a man sins against his neighbor and is made to take an oath and comes and swears his oath before your altar in this house, then hear in heaven and act and judge your servants, condemning the guilty by bringing his conduct on his own head, and vindicating the righteous by rewarding him according to his righteousness.

"When your people Israel are defeated before the enemy because they have sinned against you, and if they turn again to you and acknowledge your name and pray and plead with you in this house, then hear in heaven and forgive the sin of your people Israel and bring them again to the land that you gave to their fathers.

"When heaven is shut up and there is no rain because they have sinned against you, if they pray toward this place and acknowledge your name and turn from their sin, when you afflict them, then hear in heaven and forgive the sin of your servants, your people Israel, when you teach them the good way in which they should walk, and grant rain upon your land, which you have given to your people as an inheritance.

"If there is famine in the land, if there is pestilence or blight or mildew or locust or caterpillar, if their enemy besieges them in the land at their gates, whatever plague, whatever sickness there is, whatever prayer, whatever plea is made by any man or by all your people Israel, each knowing the affliction of his own heart and stretching out his hands toward this house, then hear in heaven your dwelling place and forgive and act and render to each whose heart you know, according to all his ways (for you, you only, know the hearts of all the children of mankind), that they may fear you all the days that they live in the land that you gave to our fathers.

"Likewise, when a foreigner, who is not of your people Israel, comes from a far country for your name's sake (for they shall hear of your great name and your mighty hand, and of your outstretched arm), when he comes and prays toward this house, hear in heaven your dwelling place and do according to all for which the foreigner calls to you, in order that all the peoples of the earth may know your name and fear you, as do your people Israel, and that they may know that this house that I have built is called by your name.

"If your people go out to battle against their enemy, by whatever way you shall send them, and they pray to the Lord toward the city that you have chosen and the house that I have built for your name, then hear in heaven their prayer and their plea, and maintain their cause.

"If they sin against you—for there is no one who does not sin—and you are angry with them and give them to an enemy, so that they are carried away captive to the land of the enemy, far off or near, yet if they turn their heart in the land to which they have been carried captive, and repent and plead with you in the land of their captors, saying, 'We have sinned and have acted perversely and wickedly,' if they repent with all their heart and with all their soul in the land of their enemies, who carried them captive, and pray to you toward their land, which you gave to their fathers, the city that you have chosen, and the house that I have built for your name, then hear in heaven your dwelling place their prayer and their plea, and maintain their cause and forgive your people who have sinned against you, and all their transgressions that they have committed against you, and grant them compassion in the sight of those who carried them captive, that they may have compassion on them (for they are your people, and your heritage, which you brought out of Egypt, from the midst of the iron furnace). Let your eyes be open to the plea of your servant and to the plea of your people Israel, giving ear to them whenever they call to you. For you separated them from among all the peoples of the earth to be your heritage, as you declared through Moses your servant, when you brought our fathers out of Egypt, O Lord God."

Now as Solomon finished offering all this prayer and plea to the Lord, he arose from before the altar of the Lord, where he had knelt with hands outstretched toward heaven. And he stood and blessed all the assembly of Israel with a loud voice, saying, "Blessed be the Lord who has given rest to his people Israel, according to all that he promised. Not one word has failed of all his good promise, which he spoke by Moses his servant. The Lord our God be with us, as he was with our fathers. May he not leave us or forsake us, that he may incline our hearts to him, to walk in all his ways and to keep his commandments, his statutes, and his rules, which he commanded our fathers. Let these words of mine, with which I have pleaded before the Lord, be near to the Lord our God day and night, and may he maintain the cause of his servant and the cause of his people Israel, as each day requires, that all the peoples of the earth may know that the Lord is God; there is no other. Let your heart therefore be wholly true to the Lord our God, walking in his statutes and keeping his commandments, as at this day."

The Fulfillment of Every Promise

The consolation of Israel was not merely Israel's victory over some political enemy. The most important part of Israel's identity, the thing that was central to its very life, was the presence of Yahweh. After the exile, during the four hundred years after Malachi's prophecies, the Hebrews did not receive a single work from their God. They had violated his laws and suffered his wrath. But God would not remain silent. He promised to fulfill his covenant to Abraham no matter how deep Israel's failures; Yahweh would complete the work he started in Israel. His people would expand beyond number; their land would become a place of peace; their enemies would be destroyed. But these amazing promises were not his people's greatest wishes. These promises were merely implications of his people's greatest desire—to live with their God in their midst. The apostle John brings all of Israel's historic anticipation and hope to bear when he penned the words that named Jesus Immanuel, God with us. In him is the fullness of God's holiness and his kindness, the final fulfillment of every promise.

THE EXODUS

The Exodus is the framework into which we must place the entire story of God and his people. The Exodus of the Hebrew people from Egypt is more than a story of an escape from a powerful enemy. It is the reversal of humanity's first exodus. In Genesis 3, God sent Adam and Eve out of his paradise and away from his life-giving presence. In Exodus 1, we see an inverted creation story: God's people live not in the freedom and plenty of a garden, but in the depravity and indignity of slavery. The story of the Scriptures clearly lays out the truth of human history—under God's rule people enjoy goodness, but under any other rule they suffer tyranny.

In Genesis 3, God comes to Moses to bring his people out of slavery and into the promised land which will begin a new exodus. It was sin that forced humanity into an exile from God, but now God would come back to his people to lead them in a new exile, this time away from evil. In this act God showed the world what return from death and sin looks like. God would save humanity from the tyrannical grasp of death in an exodus to a land that he would rule by his good and perfect government.

Genesis 3 teaches that life in this world is one of exile. The deceitful serpent does not merely introduce immoral thoughts to Eve, he alienates her from God's loving rule. Adam, Eve, and all humanity become exiles from their true home, where God ruled with loving care. On the other side of the cherubim's fiery sword people seek to replace God's rightful rule with earthly rulers who abuse power. The world refuses to admit that it is in exile from its king and so seeks to realize its own Eden. After the flood, humanity sought to make a name for itself at the tower of Babel (Genesis 11). Ancient peoples built cities in the names of idols and in Egypt the mighty Pharaohs built a tremendous empire (Exodus 1:10). Scripture tells a recurring story—humanity uses the authority gifted to them by God to build kingdoms that worship and obey created beings and things. This is the story of a world in exile.

The Exodus is the story of God bringing humanity back from exile by establishing his rightful reign against the claims of all other gods. God judges all the powers and principalities of Egypt in the ten plagues, then leads his people through the watery gate of the Red Sea. As he drove humanity out of the garden, he now leads them back into his kingdom.

But the story of redemption was not over. For the Exodus was more than freedom *from* the gods, it was freedom *to* worship and serve Yahweh. The biblical narrative clearly shows that Moses led the Hebrews out of Egypt so they might serve and worship God (Exodus 3:2). At Sinai, God's people faced the true reason for their exodus— to leave all other kings so that they might become the people of God.

While encamped at Sinai's base the Hebrews were beyond Egypt's reach, they were soon to discover that Pharaoh was not their most formidable enemy. Inside their own hearts, the Hebrews faced a darker and more pervasive oppression than they had yet known. After witnessing the mighty acts of Yahweh and watching the Red Sea collapse on Egypt's army, the Hebrews quickly returned to an idolatrous exile. With Moses gone they crafted and worshipped a golden calf (Exodus 34).

The Hebrew worship of the golden calf inaugurated an ugly cycle in Israel's history which the Old Testament recorded for posterity. Just under a year later, the Hebrews committed a treasonous act as faithless as idolatry when they refused to obey their king and cross the Jordan River. Israel stood on the brink of a new Eden, but, because of their unbelief, God punished them to forty-years of wandering in the wilderness. The Hebrews' exile back into the barren wastelands of the Sinai Peninsula was a reenactment of the four hundred years of oppression they had endured in Egypt. Over its history, Israel would suffer several exiles from its God after being blessed by exoduses out of sin and evil.

After decades, Israel finally entered the promised land-it was an event that pointed to the eventual restoration of Eden. Canaan was to be a land flowing with milk and honey, which spoke of the fruitful bounty that came from God's good rule. However, Israel once again chose to reject the redemptive work of exodus. The people gave in to idolatry time and time again until God, who had been longsuffering, finally drove them out in an exile reminiscent of Genesis 3. He empowered the fiery swords of the Assyrian Empire and then the Babylonians to drive the people from the land. In 586 BC, God punished his people by allowing he Babylonians to sack Jerusalem and destroy the temple, the seat of his presence.

By God's mercy, Israel did inhabit Jerusalem once again, but God did not return to the temple; no matter how wonderful Canaan had been, without God, it would never again be the promised land. Even in their homeland, the Hebrews lived in exile from Yahweh until the day when he would come back to his people. And even though they would rebuild the city walls, there was nothing they could do to restore their relationship with God except to wait. He would have to come to lead them on a new exodus, not out of a foreign land, but rather out of the bondage of sin and death. As with Israel in front of Sinai, neither geography nor human governments proved to be humanity's ultimate tyrants. The prophets knew that God's people would only be restored when the stripes of justice fell on the one who would be the righteous king of a holy people.

Jesus became that righteous Branch who led God's people in a new exodus out of ultimate exile in sin and death. The night before his death, Jesus ate a Passover meal with his disciples (Matthew 26); the next day, while hanging on a cross, he became the Passover lamb whose blood now stains the lintel of his people's hearts. After Passover came the Exodus. Three days later he rose from the dead, through the watery grave to lead his people on the ultimate exodus through death and to his eternal reign. We extol him, King of Kings—the only Ruler of all against all other claims to power.

DECEMBER 16

The Wisdom of God

In the beginning, God created the universe. In his telling of the universe's beginning, Moses is careful to describe creation as a process. Of course, God could have made the universe in any way he wanted, but he revealed to Moses that the world first existed as a chaotic thing. Moses does not tell us how the world came to be in this way, but he does tell us that at one point the world was "formless and void"— it had no structure and no meaning. Moses then records that over this chaos the Holy Spirit moved, then God spoke. The image of Genesis 1 and 2 is profound—on its own the universe had no order but rather received order from outside itself. God spoke to give the universe order, purpose, and beauty.

In the fall, Adam and Eve exchanged God's word for Satan's word. At one time they were called to transform the rest of the globe into a garden on Eden's blueprint, but Adan and Eve's sin consigned them to work in broken, disordered ground. But sin not only subjected human beings to difficult lives, but it also twisted their minds to believe that they could order the world best if they worked independently from and in opposition to their Creator.

Because they bear their Creator's image, humans have developed technical abilities in art, construction, agriculture, and war. They became adept at arranging the parts and pieces of the world around them to build kingdoms and cultures which reveal, although only in part, the glory of God. Apart from him, however, human genius only confirms the broken logic of a broken world, a formlessness that cannot give people that for which they most deeply yearn—true meaning. Adam and Eve's descendants made astounding accomplishments, but none of them have ended their exile from their Creator's embrace. Without the word of God, all human effort results in the grave.

Through the burning bush, Yahweh revealed to Moses the meaninglessness of human genius. The Egyptians had certainly constructed one of the greatest civilizations in the history of the world. And yet its splendor was a temporary statue to imagined gods. Against the doomed wonders of that pagan empire, Yahweh revealed himself to Moses as the eternal and absolute truth above and through all things.

Throughout the Bible's first five books, Yahweh introduces to the Hebrews a new understanding of human life. Ourselves, our neighbors, and our world only receive meaning from him. Apart from him, all of man's works only reveal the formlessness and void of Genesis 1:1. This truth proved hard for the Hebrews, a ragtag people living in the shadow of Egypt's might, to understand. The vanity of human power must have been difficult for Israel to see when they were overwhelmed by the strength of empires like Assyria and Babylon. For all their greatness, the kingdoms of man are futile. In serving this world, they are all slaves to the disorder of death that comes to individuals and civilizations alike. To a world disordered by death, Yahweh gives humanity his something more valuable than all the splendor of human achievement—wisdom.

The author of Proverbs defines wisdom as the fear of the Lord, which reveals something central to God's view of humanity. People live their lives in fear either of the Lord or of something else. Since the fall people have feared death, not just physical death but also the ruin that comes to everything people value. God was clear in the curse—all things in this world return to dust. To a world in which all things die, Yahweh speaks. He speaks and chaos became order. He speaks and death becomes life. It is foolish to live according to any words other than God's, while wisdom is the commitment to live by the same word of God that separated light from dark, and land from sea at the very beginning. Wisdom is the way one lives when one believes that death, and all its many consequences, is a powerless thing next to the infinite goodness and unmeasurable power of Yahweh.

All too often Israel conceded to the foolishness of this world, even though God not only taught them truth but also demonstrated it. The Hebrews feared other governments, giants in Canaan, and drought. They turned to the science of their day to give their lives meaning. They committed acts that made sense in a world that is trying to avoid death, but that are evil in the sight of Yahweh. In his grace, God revealed to his people the truth beyond what their eyes could see. Walking in the ways of this world only takes people down the wide path to destruction. And even though God's word appears foolish to this world, it is the only path that leads to life.

PROVERBS 8

Does not wisdom call?

Does not understanding raise her voice? On the heights beside the way, at the crossroads she takes her stand; beside the gates in front of the town, at the entrance of the portals she cries aloud:

"To you, O men, I call, and my cry is to the children of man. O simple ones, learn prudence; O fools, learn sense. Hear, for I will speak noble things, and from my lips will come what is right, for my mouth will utter truth; wickedness is an abomination to my lips. All the words of my mouth are righteous; there is nothing twisted or crooked in them. They are all straight to him who understands, and right to those who find knowledge. Take my instruction instead of silver, and knowledge rather than choice gold, for wisdom is better than jewels, and all that you may desire cannot compare with her.

"I, wisdom, dwell with prudence, and I find knowledge and discretion.

The fear of the Lord is hatred of evil. Pride and arrogance and the way of evil and perverted speech I hate. I have counsel and sound wisdom; I have insight; I have strength. By me kings reign, and rulers decree what is just; by me princes' rule, and nobles, all who govern justly.

I love those who love me, and those who seek me diligently find me. Riches and honor are with me, enduring wealth and righteousness. My fruit is better than gold, even fine gold, and my yield than choice silver. I walk in the way of righteousness, in the paths of justice, granting an inheritance to those who love me and filling their treasuries.

"The Lord possessed me at the beginning of his work, the first of his acts of old. Ages ago I was set up, at the first, before the beginning of the earth. When there were no depths, I was brought forth, when there were no springs abounding with water. Before the mountains had been shaped, before the hills, I was brought forth, before he had made the earth with its fields, or the first of the dust of the world. When he established the heavens, I was there; when he drew a circle on the face of the deep, when he made firm the skies above, when he established the fountains of the deep, when he assigned to the sea its limit, so that the waters might not transgress his command, when he marked out the foundations of the earth, then I was beside him, like a master workman, and I was daily his delight, rejoicing before him always, rejoicing in his inhabited world and delighting in the children of man.

"And now, O sons, listen to me: blessed are those who keep my ways. Hear instruction and be wise, and do not neglect it.

Blessed is the one who listens to me, watching daily at my gates, waiting beside my doors. For whoever finds me finds life and obtains favor from the Lord, but he who fails to find me injures himself; all who hate me love death."

Fear of the Lord

To fear the Lord is to live for the eternal love of our heavenly Father. As it did for Israel, wisdom presents God's people with difficult challenges. Fallen humanity seeks success on the terms of this temporary world. On the other hand, the Church desires faithful loyalty to an eternal city under God's reign, even if doing so means failing in this temporal life. By all worldly measures, God's people have never been successful-to this world Christians are foolish. To make matters worse, the head of the Church himself was a failed leader who was executed as a common criminal. But in the very experience that shows a man at his weakest—death—Jesus exhibited a power beyond human imagination. He rose. He worked the disorder of death backwards when he conquered the grave. In his resurrection Christ revealed the same awesome power he had exerted at creation and confirmed Yahweh's wisdom against all the foolishness of man. He is the greatest power in the universe, the King over all reality. Trust in him; love him; obey him; fear him and fear nothing else—this is wisdom.

DECEMBER 17

The Promise of a Son

Death is exile; exile is death. All the cultures in world history have found a place for death. For the Ancient Near East, it was a transition from one plane to another; for the Ancient Greeks it was a movement from the upper world to the lower world. In Asia, death has been an escape from the world of pain to a world of nothing, or the embarkation onto a cycle of lives. God is clear death is exile from the Creator because of sin. The home for humanity is in the presence of the author of life, the only true God in whom there is no darkness and no evil. Any movement away from him is a move towards the unnatural place of an exile humans experience as death.

But death is more profound than just the end of physical life. Scripture teaches that all human suffering and loss is merely an extension of death. For Paul, death touches our lives with sin as it reaches back from the grave to pull us into its final grip. Sin is a wage we earn or a payment towards the final mortgage of death. (Romans 6:23) Seen this way, the exile of the Hebrews from the land of Israel was an extension of the grave—the physical reality of ultimate separation from Yahweh.

To see the world this way required the Hebrews to deny every urge to agree with the world in which they lived. Death is not the failure of strength, and Israel's military defeat was not the result of strategic failure. The gods did not triumph while Yahweh failed. Rather, loss to the Assyrians and then the Babylonians was another consequence of sin against God. Israel's defeat was another instance of the fall after temptation which has played itself out in the individual and corporate lives of God's people since Cain killed Abel.

The relationship between death and exile from God reveals the true nature of reality. Most people see the world as a battle between good and evil. Throughout history, human cultures have seen good and bad things in this world as spillover from an unseen battle between gods. In modern times many people, especially in the West, see history as a battle between good people and bad people. Bad things result from the bad side winning; good things result from the good side winning.

We have been thoroughly catechized to see our lives as a battle between light and dark. But the Scriptures reveal a very different reality. There is no power in the universe that can oppose Yahweh. He is not in a battle with evil. Rather bad things are, in some dimension, a judgment on all sin against God, while every good thing comes from God's character. Israel did not fall because it picked the wrong god. Rather, Israel entered darkness because it disobeyed the God of light and life. In other words, while Assyria was the rod of God's judgment, Assyria were not Israel's ultimate enemy.

The Hebrews, Scripture makes clear, were their own enemies. They had rejected Yahweh's kingship as they sought out other gods. They exiled themselves spiritually and politically from God which led to their physical exile from their homeland. It was the evil in their hearts that plunged them into darkness. Thus, coming back from exile would not result from winning a battle or gaining the friendship of a different, more powerful god. Only Yahweh himself could lead Israel back from exile. The Hebrews needed forgiveness, not a better military. They needed grace, not better tactics.

God foresaw that his people would repeat Eve's sin over and over throughout their history. The Bible is not careful to protect the reputation of God's people. It reveals, in terrible detail, the fateful decisions of the Patriarchs, the Hebrew peoples, and their rulers. Hoping to end the pain of exile, people reject Yahweh and refuse to follow him on an exodus from sin. They would rather call their exile home and home with Yahweh exile.

Despite his people's nearly constant temptation to sin, however, God planned to redeem them from themselves. He would not wait for them to save themselves but would raise up a king from among them. The pattern he laid down from the very beginning was to bring new life by his own doing, a life that he would use to bring his people back from their own self-imposed exile. He brought Adam and Eve a child after the Abel's violent death. Seth kept the seed of the woman and, therefore, the promises of God alive. He gave Isaac to Sarah and Abraham—the child of promise. He called Samuel into the temple to serve him, and he marked David out as the leader of his people.

As the Hebrews faced their deepest and harshest exile, God confirmed not only his promise from Genesis 3 but his plan to redeem his people from themselves. Through a child, God would build a government that would provide all the benefits that flow from a restored relationship with him. This great promise confirms the Bible's view of reality. All good comes from a right relationship with Yahweh, all evil results from a broken relationship with Yahweh. In his mercy, Yahweh would do what his people could not. By his own power he would restore the relationship with his people in a political establishment that would end their exile forever.

ISAIAH 9:2-7

The people who walked in darkness
 have seen a great light;
those who dwelt in a land of deep darkness,
 on them has light shone.
You have multiplied the nation;
 you have increased its joy;
they rejoice before you
 as with joy at the harvest,
 as they are glad when they divide the spoil.
For the yoke of his burden,
 and the staff for his shoulder,
 the rod of his oppressor,
 you have broken as on the day of Midian.
For every boot of the tramping warrior in battle tumult
 and every garment rolled in blood
 will be burned as fuel for the fire.
For to us a child is born,
 to us a son is given;
and the government shall be upon his shoulder,
 and his name shall be called
Wonderful Counselor, Mighty God,
 Everlasting Father, Prince of Peace.
Of the increase of his government and of peace
 there will be no end,
on the throne of David and over his kingdom,
 to establish it and to uphold it
with justice and with righteousness
 from this time forth and forevermore.
The zeal of the Lord of hosts will do this.

The Only Son of God

To human eyes, the world looked just the same after Jesus came as it did before he was born. No matter who his disciples claimed he was, Rome still occupied the known world while the Sanhedrin remained a defeated Jewish government. To the people of first century Palestine, Jesus himself looked like an ordinary man. He ate when hungry, walked dusty roads, and wore carpenter's clothes. Despite what people saw with their eyes or heard with their ears, Jesus' birth upended the world because it inaugurated the world's exodus from exile to a relationship with its Creator.

Even his disciples did not fully understand this reality. But to Peter, James, and John, Jesus disclosed true reality. Before their eyes he peeled back his cultural garb and took on the royal robes of his divinity in what the Gospel writers called the Transfiguration. Above the cowering disciples, Jesus met with Elijah and Moses.

Elijah was God's prophet to his people in exile; Moses was the man God chose to lead Israel on its exodus out of Egypt. While he looked like a normal, mortal man, Jesus was the King who would lead his people on an exodus from their exile of death to new life with the Father. In the pattern of all his promises, God inaugurated his plan of redemption with the birth of a son, heir to the promises and guarantor of restoration for all his people.

DECEMBER 18

He Bore Our Sins

Sin brought death to humanity. Sin is both the natural consequence of alienation from God and the just judgment on those who reject his kingship. The consequences of sin have been terrible in human history. People are locked in a struggle with the natural world which will result in their death and its ruination. Disease infiltrates communities while humans commit crimes against one another. Despite our best efforts to fix the human condition, it has and will be defined by corruption.

But the Bible provides hope to humanity's very dark and difficult reality. The death that resulted from sin is also the very tool that God has determined to use to destroy corruption, end sin, and restore humanity to life under his reign. The first thing that God did after proclaiming the curse over Adam and Eve was to kill an animal in order to cover his people with its death. Their son then built his relationship with God on his faithful sacrifices. Abel offered the best of what he had to the Lord. God's response to Abel is amazing: "The Lord had regard for Abel and his offering." (Genesis 4:4) Adam and Eve were exiled from the garden for breaking their relationship with God. But by his sacrifices, Abel was re-forging that relationship.

From the very first sacrifice, the relationship between God and his people has been built on sacrifice. By death God defied death. What sin destroyed, sacrifices to God rebuilt, if only in part. Yet God seemed to leave this plan vague in the minds of the Hebrews until he handed down his law at Sinai. He prepared to fulfill his greatest promise by making himself a home among his people. It would be the sacrifices for sin that would make this possible. Over this system, God placed a carefully chosen and trained priesthood. These priests would see that the sacrifices, among other rituals, were performed according to God's laws. God set in motion a plan that would heal his relationship with his people from death by using death itself.

In conjunction with the priesthood, God planned to give Israel someone who would lead the people in obeying God's moral laws. Moses took on this role, while the sons of Aaron took on the roles of priests. Together they set a pattern for living with Yahweh—sacrifices for a sinful people and moral law to direct their life together in his presence. Right from the beginning, however, the plan faltered because of the enduring presence of sin. Leaders failed and priests abused the sacrificial system by corrupting it in service to other gods. Without priests and leaders functioning as God had designed them to function, the hope of redemption shattered into exile and a death that does not restore.

Solomon's sins against Yahweh were the blow that seemed to destroy any hope of Israel living in a restored relationship with its God. The king, God's chosen leader, abandoned the moral law. The priests under Solomon turned to idols so that they might make peace with this world; they instead made themselves enemies of their God. Without the right use of death in the sacrificial system, Israel experienced a total separation from Yahweh at the hands of the Assyrians and the Babylonians. Exile was death without redemption. It seemed that God's promises had failed because God's people had failed. In their despair, Israel missed the deeper truths of God's plan. He always planned to redeem his people, and through them the world—by his own might, his own goodness, and his own glory.

What Israel did not understand is that the priesthood he created and the leaders he called were not meant to be the ones who finally restored his relationship to Israel. Rather, these were only models that would help his people understand how God would finally redeem his people. For Yahweh revealed through Isaiah a remarkable plan. God would draw together the role of the priest and the position of the king together into one person who himself would become the restoration of Israel. God's plan may have seemed to fail when Samuel's children abandoned right worship and Solomon married foreign wives. Yet neither Aaron, Moses, Samuel, David, nor Solomon were ever the keys to his plan—they were only examples which he used to train the Hebrews' hearts and minds on the one who would in fact be their redemption.

God would raise up a king who would keep all his moral law, in a way that no human king on his own could ever do. This king would then present himself as the final sacrifice for his people. He would attend to all the rituals God instituted for the preparation of the sacrifice, then offer his own life to God. What all the animal sacrifices over generations pointed toward but could not fulfill, this final sacrifice would accomplish. God's king would die to destroy death; he would then rule over a people who could finally live in the presence of their God.

ISAIAH 52:13–53:12

Behold, my servant shall act wisely; he shall be high and lifted up and shall be exalted.

As many were astonished at you—

his appearance was so marred, beyond human semblance,

and his form beyond that of the children of mankind— so shall he sprinkle many nations. Kings shall shut their mouths because of him, for that which has not been told them they see, and that which they have not heard they understand.

Who has believed what he has heard from us

And to whom has the arm of the Lord been revealed? For he grew up before him like a young plant, and like a root out of dry ground; he had no form or majesty that we should look at him, and no beauty that we should desire him. He was despised and rejected by men, a man of sorrows and acquainted with grief; and as one from whom men hide their faces he was despised, and we esteemed him not.

Surely he has borne our griefs and carried our sorrows; yet we esteemed him stricken, smitten by God, and afflicted. But he was pierced for our transgressions; he was crushed for our iniquities; upon him was the chastisement that brought us peace, and with his wounds we are healed. All we like sheep have gone astray; we have turned—everyone—to his own way; and the Lord has laid on him the iniquity of us all.

He was oppressed, and he was afflicted, yet he opened not his mouth; like a lamb that is led to the slaughter, and like a sheep that before its shearers is silent, so he opened not his mouth.

By oppression and judgment he was taken away; and as for his generation, who considered that he was cut off out of the land of the living, stricken for the transgression of my people? And they made his grave with the wicked and with a rich man in his death, although he had done no violence, and there was no deceit in his mouth.

Yet it was the will of the Lord to crush him; he has put him to grief; when his soul makes an offering for guilt, he shall see his offspring; he shall prolong his days; the will of the Lord shall prosper in his hand.

Out of the anguish of his soul he shall see and be satisfied;
by his knowledge shall the righteous one, my servant, make many
to be accounted righteous, and he shall bear their iniquities.

Therefore I will divide him a portion with the many, and he
shall divide the spoil with the strong, because he poured out his
soul to death and was numbered with the transgressors; yet he
bore the sin of many and makes intercession for the transgressors.

King Over All Kings

Pilate understood the danger that Christ presented. Jesus presented a crisis to the Sanhedrin which used the Torah's sacrificial
system as a political tool to manage the Jewish people. The priests
of first-century Jerusalem abused God's law in order to secure political victory. For all their religious garb and practices, they lacked
interest in the one thing that the sacrificial system was meant to
secure—right relationship with Yahweh. They convinced Pilate to
execute Jesus by saying that he was a king. In that place and time,
any king became a rival to Caesar and so must suffer execution at
the hands of the Romans.

Pilate asked Jesus, "Are you a king?" The question must have
seemed absurd to Pilate, who asked it of a broken and bloodied
teacher. Jesus could not even secure his disciples' loyalty in a
moment of crisis. How could he possibly be a king? What Pilate
could not see was that in the moment of his suffering and death,
Jesus became the king that Yahweh had always promised: the king
who became death to destroy death so that he might restore his
people's relationship to God. In his resurrection he asserted his
royal reign over all time, all peoples, all worlds.

DECEMBER 19

The People Saw a Great Light

The world lies in darkness. This seems like a strange thing to say about so many different peoples and nations. Surely different societies and cultures shed light on this world through art, science, technology, and philosophy. Civilizations bear the marks of human genius as they make life-changing advances. But the Scriptures are clear—the only light is that which directs mankind back to the Creator. All good things are only good in service to a loving relationship with Yahweh. No human effort, no matter how brilliant, has reversed the curse of sin; the strength of humanity is no match for the grave.

But God did not leave the world without a witness. He called out a slave nation to become a mirror across which his light would dawn for all of humanity. He rescued them from their worldly captors and invested in them his holy law, which would clear the thorny ground for his arrival back into this broken world. It was clear through the Exodus that with Yahweh was the power of life. Unlike all the other gods who competed for control, Yahweh revealed himself as God alone. From the bush that would not burn, Yahweh named himself, "I am who I am." (Exodus 3:14) In a world in which all authority and position relied upon a proper lineage, Yahweh claimed to be the source of his own authority. In calling himself "I am," Yahweh claimed to be the source of all authority on heaven and on earth. He is the source of all light and goodness wherever it may be found. Without Yahweh the world is covered in thick darkness.

God gave Israel the highest calling of any nation in history: to reflect the light of Yahweh on the world and so dispel the darkness. But Israel failed. Its people chose the darkness of idolatry over the light of Yahweh. From the five lords of the Philistines to the unstoppable power of the Babylonian empire, God handed Israel over to its desires. He took away the light of his presence and consigned Israel to the darkness that enshrouds every other nation. Its precious possessions were dispersed to more powerful kingdoms. The walls that represented Israel's glory and strength were reduced to rubble. Unable to protect its people, Jerusalem became a dangerous place. Villains could break in at any time to despoil whoever tried to hide in its ruins. In the ancient world a place like Jerusalem became a byword, a joke, one of those places that becomes a parable of weakness and dishonor.

In the world's mind, the reason for Israel's failure was easy to understand: Israel lacked the proper strength. Its leaders could not appeal to the right gods. The city was poorly defended, and its people were weak. Israel offered no help to other nations who were trying to hold on to their own safety. The only reason that people would look to Israel was to learn how not to mount a defense against enemy powers. By all earthly standards Israel was powerless; worse, Israel was useless.

But God did not want Israel to be an example of strength—he created it to be the model of faithfulness to him. Israel failed not because it lacked military strength. It lacked military strength because it did not love Yahweh. If the world had eyes to see, they would have learned that success in this world is not the ultimate goal of living. Rather, success is a consequence of doing the most important thing in the world, which is loving the Lord God. Had Israel understood that it would have become what the world always needed—an example of God's love and grace. Restored by Yahweh, Israel would have been a light to all nations whose brightness would the world the depth of its darkness.

Though Israel fell to the military strength of her worldly enemies, God promised that he would one day bring light back to Israel. In what would be a cosmic reversal, Yahweh promised to restore light to Israel so that by it, Israel's captors would come back to God. By the world's wisdom, Midian and Ephah, Tarshish and Lebanon were all enemies of Israel's safety. But by the grace of Yahweh, Israel's enemies would become servants to his light. For God will not rest until all the world brings to him its treasures. The nations of the world, still in darkness, do not yet understand that without Yahweh all their great wealth is little more than dust in the early stages of decay. But in service to the eternal king, all good things in this world become eternally valuable. Thus, the presence of Yahweh himself will make Israel so beautiful that every other nation will seek to bring all the valuable riches they own as sacrifices to him, so that they might be part of his people.

The world does not realize it, but right relationship with Yahweh is the ultimate good that it desires. To see this truth is to make all the good things of this world pale in comparison. And yet once the world sees this truth, all the good things of this world begin to make sense. They are mere consequences of humanity's relationship with Yahweh restored. To this light every nation will come. All peoples will stream to this truth, for by it all that is right and good in this world makes sense.

ISAIAH 60

Arise, shine, for your light has come, and the glory of the Lord has risen upon you. For behold, darkness shall cover the earth, and thick darkness the peoples; but the Lord will arise upon you, and his glory will be seen upon you. And nations shall come to your light, and kings to the brightness of your rising.

Lift up your eyes all around, and see; they all gather together, they come to you; your sons shall come from afar, and your daughters shall be carried on the hip. Then you shall see and be radiant; your heart shall thrill and exult, because the abundance of the sea shall be turned to you, the wealth of the nations shall come to you. A multitude of camels shall cover you, the young camels of Midian and Ephah; all those from Sheba shall come. They shall bring gold and frankincense, and shall bring good news, the praises of the Lord. All the flocks of Kedar shall be gathered to you; the rams of Nebaioth shall minister to you; they shall come up with acceptance on my altar, and I will beautify my beautiful house.

Who are these that fly like a cloud, and like doves to their windows? For the coastlands shall hope for me, the ships of Tarshish first, to bring your children from afar, their silver and gold with them, for the name of the Lord your God, and for the Holy One of Israel, because he has made you beautiful.

Foreigners shall build up your walls, and their kings shall minister to you; for in my wrath, I struck you, but in my favor I have had mercy on you. Your gates shall be open continually; day and night they shall not be shut, that people may bring to you the wealth of the nations, with their kings led in procession. For the nation and kingdom that will not serve you shall perish; those nations shall be utterly laid waste. The glory of Lebanon shall come to you, the cypress, the plane, and the pine, to beautify the place of my sanctuary, and I will make the place of my feet glorious. The sons of those who afflicted you shall come bending low to you, and all who despised you shall bow down at your feet; they shall call you the City of the Lord, the Zion of the Holy One of Israel.

Whereas you have been forsaken and hated, with no one passing through, I will make you majestic forever, a joy from age to age. You shall suck the milk of nations; you shall nurse at the breast of kings; and you shall know that I, the Lord, am your Savior and your Redeemer, the Mighty One of Jacob.

Instead of bronze I will bring gold, and instead of iron I will bring silver, instead of wood, bronze, instead of stones, iron. I will make your overseers peace and your taskmasters' righteousness. Violence shall no more be heard in your land, devastation or destruction within your borders; you shall call your walls Salvation, and your gates Praise.

The sun shall be no more your light by day, nor for brightness shall the moon give you light; but the Lord will be your everlasting light, and your God will be your glory. Your sun shall no more go down, nor your moon withdraw itself; for the Lord will be your everlasting light, and your days of mourning shall be ended. Your people shall all be righteous; they shall possess the land forever, the branch of my planting, the work of my hands, that I might be glorified. The least one shall become a clan, and the smallest one a mighty nation; I am the Lord; in its time I will hasten it.

The Light from God

Jesus Christ, the only true light, came into a world covered in darkness. Through the Exodus, the giving of the law, and the construction of the priesthood, God made Israel a shard that would reflect his light into darkened nations. But his people failed to train their lives on Yahweh and so became dark themselves, so dark that they could not recognize the light himself. Jesus is the one in whom the fullness of the Godhead dwells among the people of this world. He is the fulfillment of all God's promises to restore mankind back to himself. In him all the beauty and treasure of this world finally makes sense, since he is the author and sustainer of all things. He is the one who makes all things good. The world without him lies in darkness, a darkness so complete that the grave itself is the only possible metaphor.

DECEMBER 20

The Reign of Justice

God had given his people many pictures of the redemption he promised. To Abraham, he promised descendants so great that they would outnumber the sands on the seashore. Through Moses, Yahweh promised to build a nation which would command a new Eden. David recorded that one-day God's appointed king would sit on Israel's throne forever. Running through all these promises was a two-part reality. First, by these different agents God promised to bring the world back to himself so that it would one day follow his good order. Second, Yahweh would defeat the seed of the serpent, and with it all the consequences of sin and death. Restoration would follow victory.

The peoples of the Ancient Near East understood that victory was military success. Israel had every reason to think the same way. To prepare Canaan for the coming of God's presence, Israel needed to defeat all the peoples in the land with armies. After the death of Joshua, Israel fell victim to foreign armies. Israel only knew peace after the victories of God's appointed judges, when Hebrew armies defeated their captors. In the years of the divided kingdom, an average Hebrew living in Judah would understand that the northern kingdom had fallen to a mighty an army that Israel could not defeat.

If victory resulted from the strength of armies, then strength of arms granted the winner political, social, and cultural control of the enemy. Total control of a people is called hegemony—that is, the power not only to control a people's resources, but to determine the way they live their lives. To be conquered, in many cases, meant having to live like your captor. Warlike peoples transformed conquered lands into warlike empires. The character of the victors determined the culture of the lands they conquered.

It was natural for ancient peoples, as it is for modern people, to believe that because military might lead to conquest, military cultures were superior. The political and social systems that made a people powerful should be the same systems that defined culture. In this way, enslaving foreign peoples became the centerpiece of most societies. Thus, many cultures in the Ancient Near East were defined by a particular military and political genius. Israel learned to expect Yahweh's redemption to look the same as any other victory. Many Hebrews of the ancient period, as with Jews during the Hasmonean period and the time under Roman occupation, defined Yahweh's redemption in the terms of their day. Israel's armies would defeat her enemies and subjugate foreign peoples, so that they could build a militarized state. Israel's political dominance would signal Yahweh's victory.

But God promised nearly the exact inverse of what most people in the Ancient Near East, including the Hebrews, would have expected. While God promised that his plan of redemption included the defeat of his enemies, he revealed that the purpose of that victory would be to create shalom in the world, not a culture of war. Unlike all other kings who became slaves to the violent tactics that brought them into power, Yahweh claimed to be the King above all other kings. For Yahweh, military violence would not define his hegemonic reign, but rather mercy would be the means of his great victory. His conquests would not display a character of military conquest; they would be characterized instead by his work of redemption.

The kingdom of Yahweh would not be an unjust culture of military conquest. Rather, Yahweh's victory over the nations would come by the establishment of justice upon the earth. It was the serpent's lie in Eden that reversed God's plan for his cosmos. As Eve took the fruit into her own hands because it seemed good for food, so all the people since the fall have taken power in this world to do what seems right to them. What seems irrational to fallen people is the very nature of Yahweh's reign over all creation. Eden seems as irrational to us now as the world now would have appeared to Adam and Eve before the fall.

That God would bring redemption through victory made sense to the Hebrews, but that Yahweh would establish justice through victory was too radical for them to understand. The military prowess of most civilizations made social injustices permanent characteristics of their societies. But Yahweh's reign would be defined by the elimination of injustice. The poor would not be obstacles to military power, but rather the beneficiaries of his power. Enslaving captive peoples was the essence of political control. But Yahweh would establish his power to free captives, bring dignity to slaves, and restore the marginalized. In order to remain strong enough to ensure military dominance, nearly all the nations forced the sick and infirmed to the fringes of society. But Yahweh would make the care of the sick and infirm the defining feature of his kingdom.

ISAIAH 61

The Spirit of the Lord God is upon me, because the Lord has anointed me to bring good news to the poor; he has sent me to bind up the brokenhearted, to proclaim liberty to the captives, and the opening of the prison to those who are bound; to proclaim the year of the Lord's favor, and the day of vengeance of our God; to comfort all who mourn; to grant to those who mourn in Zion— to give them a beautiful headdress instead of ashes, the oil of gladness instead of mourning, the garment of praise instead of a faint spirit; that they may be called oaks of righteousness, the planting of the Lord, that he may be glorified. They shall build up the ancient ruins; they shall raise up the former devastations; they shall repair the ruined cities, the devastations of many generations.

Strangers shall stand and tend your flocks; foreigners shall be your plowmen and vinedressers; but you shall be called the priests of the Lord; they shall speak of you as the ministers of our God; you shall eat the wealth of the nations, and in their glory you shall boast.

Instead of your shame there shall be a double portion; instead of dishonor they shall rejoice in their lot; therefore in their land they shall possess a double portion; they shall have everlasting joy.

For I the Lord love justice; I hate robbery and wrong; I will faithfully give them their recompense, and I will make an everlasting covenant with them. Their offspring shall be known among the nations, and their descendants in the midst of the peoples; all who see them shall acknowledge them, that they are an offspring the Lord has blessed.

I will greatly rejoice in the Lord; my soul shall exult in my God, for he has clothed me with the garments of salvation; he has covered me with the robe of righteousness, as a bridegroom decks himself like a priest with a beautiful headdress, and as a bride adorns herself with her jewels. For as the earth brings forth its sprouts, and as a garden causes what is sown in it to sprout up, so the Lord God will cause righteousness and praise to sprout up before all the nations.

A Kingdom of Justice

Up until the time that Jesus appeared in public after his baptism in the Jordan and after his time of temptation in the wilderness, only a few people had any idea who he was. Although the king of creation walked among them, people only saw a boy, a teenager, and then a young man. He bore none of the characteristics of a warrior leader. He did not train to fight, nor did he exhibit political genius. Other than an aging priest and an old prophetess, no one mistook Jesus for one who could conquer Rome in order to make Israel a formidable military state. In the terms of the fallen world, Jesus had no chance of bringing Israel victory.

But in the wilderness, he resisted the great liar who offered him military might and power. His kingship was that of redemption, not of petty things like political victory. He entered the synagogue as the redeemer king who would conquer through justice, not control societies for military purposes. Before a packed house, Jesus spoke a new world into existence, a world that had not existed since Eve sampled the fruit. Jesus inaugurated a rule of love, mercy, and justice that would, by the Holy Spirit, restore all the world to himself.

THE SACRIFICE

All people seek the way back to Eden's Garden and thus back into a loving relationship with their Creator. Philosophers and priests, scientists and bureaucrats have long sought to build their own roads to utopia and heaven. God has marked that path, but the world cannot accept it. Only through sacrificial death will life finally be restored. Death is not only the one universal characteristic of life after the fall, but it is also the only door that leads back to our Creator. In his mercy, God used the very punishment for sin as the means by which he would bring humanity back into Eden.

God warned Adam and Eve about the consequences of violating his commandment regarding the tree of the knowledge of good and evil. By eating of that tree, they would exchange God's word, the only source of life, for the word of Satan, the author of lies. While his warning was at one level a supernatural judgment, at another level, it simply drew attention to the fabric of existence. God sustains all things; therefore, rejecting his reign is the same as destroying life. In the poetry of the creation story, sin moves the world back to the formlessness and void of Genesis 1:2, before God's word brought order and life.

In Genesis 3 God confirmed for Adam and Eve the terrible price of their treachery. They would surely die. But rather than allow death to do its terrible work, God commuted Adam and Eve's punishment. Although they would die, God sustained their lives for a season by the word of his promise. Then he went farther. In his great mercy, he not only granted Adam and Eve a reprieve from death, but he also created a road back to life again. After delivering the sentence for their terrible sin, God covered Adam and Eve with animal skins. The first death recorded in the Scriptures came from God's own hand, as he sacrificed an innocent animal to ensure his people's lives. In that instance, God transformed the very punishment owed to sinners into the only way back to relationship with him.

The world accepts neither God's judgment for sin nor the way he has marked out for its elimination. The world has always sought to avoid death. Better governments, laws, and technology all promise to extend life as long as possible or even to avoid the grave altogether. The Scriptures, however, explain two inescapable truths: since the fall there is no life without death, and death is the only path that leads back to God. God taught Israel these truths slowly and progressively, beginning with the bloody skin that he draped over Adam and Eve's naked shoulders. He demonstrated the importance of sacrifice again just one chapter later with the faithful offerings Abel made to his God. These simple stories formed the broad foundation upon which God built the tradition and theology of sacrifice as the only way of redemption.

In the sacrificial practices he inaugurated for Israel, God redeemed the very evil that Adam and Eve brought upon the world.

Through sacrifice God makes death itself the way he restores life. God confirmed the necessary and beautiful role of sacrifice when he called on Abraham to kill his only son Isaac. God made a promise of abundant life to Abraham when he said that Abraham's children would become a nation whose people could not be numbered. To fulfill this promise, God gave Abraham a son, Isaac, as the only one through whom this promise would be fulfilled. In Genesis 22, God did the unthinkable when he commanded Abraham to sacrifice Isaac on an altar.

Certainly, Isaac's death would have meant the end of God's mighty promises. When God stopped Abraham from plunging the knife through Isaac's heart, God taught Israel the meaning of sacrificial death: "By myself I have sworn, declares the Lord, because you have done this and have not withheld your son, your only son, I will surely bless you, and I will surely multiply your offspring as the stars of heaven and as the sand that is on the seashore." (Genesis 22:16–17)

The angel of the Lord stopped Abraham's hand only because in his heart Abraham had already taken his son's life. The bloodless sacrifice of Isaac was the very act through which God would fulfill his promises. But death was still the only way of redemption, and so in Isaac's stead God provided a ram which served as an emblem of Yahweh's gracious provision. Nearly two thousand years later, God the Father would walk his son to a cross but there would be no ram.

In Moses' law, God continued to teach Israel that only through the blood and pain of sacrifice would he restore his people to loving communion. Moses patterned Israel's calendar on a system of sacrifices and feasts that kept before them the terrible cost of sin and also the mercy of God, who would use death to defeat death. It seems that Israel never fully grasped the deep importance of atoning sacrifices. Once they were in the promised land they aban-

doned God's redemption for the life-ending sacrifices demanded by
Baal and Molech. Death regained its awful power to end life. In the
depth of Israel's fall from God's promises, Isaiah saw the coming
of a new sacrifice—one who would die for his people and so transform death into new life.

DECEMBER 21

Laws Written on the Heart

Yahweh judged his people for treason against his rule. While
all governments use a similar power to constrain threats to their
power, Yahweh's judgments are pure. He did not rule over Israel to
expand his own power—he covenanted with Israel so that together,
king and people, they might work to restore the world back to
Yahweh. Yet the Hebrews chafed under his laws. They found his
holiness too strange. The Hebrews had forgotten why Yahweh had
made them a nation. The nation was not the point of Yahweh's
kingship but a framework which would allow Israel to live in a
relationship with Yahweh. This relationship was supposed to be so
central to Israel that God often referred to it as a marriage—that
intimate relationship that defines one's entire life. But Israel
rejected their God in order to become a nation like every other
nation. God scattered his people to take their idols from them and
teach them once again that their true purpose in this world was to
love the Lord their God with their hearts, minds, and souls.

But living to love Yahweh is a so strange to a fallen world that
few understand or pursue it. Throughout Scripture, God refers to

this way of living as the narrow way and the few who move along its difficult path a remnant—a strange band of people navigate a very difficult road in obedience to Yahweh, while the rest of the world together comfortably walks the wide paved road to destruction. Yahweh marked out this strange pathway with the covenant he handed down to Moses.

On the stone tablets, God scribed a way of life in service to him that would make Israel different than all the other nations. In their faithfulness to their covenant with Yahweh, Israel would appear to be a very peculiar people. While other nations used their relationships to the gods to secure peace and prosperity, Israel would reject the gods in order to bless the nations. Rather than participate in the activities which normally led to a secure nation, the Hebrews would organize their entire lives around bizarre cultural system based on weird sacrifices.

Even for the Jews, the law of Yahweh proved too strange. God had promised to redeem the world through a people under his government. The law defined Israel as a nation; the Davidic kings gave Israel the necessary administration. More than that, God validated his kingship over them through miracles that were beyond explanation. He gave Israel examples of those who resisted his kingship, from foreign enemies he defeated to Hebrews that he judged. And yet, other than a few faithful generations, the people of Israel returned to the gods that they knew.

Government and law failed; Yahweh's kingship did not fail. With the people enslaved by foreign nations, the hope that God would restore the nation of Israel under the old covenant seemed impossible. The covenants from Moses to David seemed to entail a functioning government, which could administer a law system over a people who occupied a physical land. It made sense, therefore, that to restore the covenant Yahweh would work this broken situation in reverse. He would conquer the land, call back his people, restore the law, and anoint a new government. The Hebrews cultivated a hope that God would restore the old covenant in all its political dimensions.

Yahweh revealed that while the restoration of his kingship was the final goal of his redemption, the national mechanism of that redemption was temporary. For many Hebrews this revelation would prove more difficult than even the Mosaic and Davidic systems he instituted. For Yahweh promised to restore his kingship by working his law not through a governmental apparatus, but rather directly through the hearts of his people.

God's kingship is of a different sort than all other governments. The Hebrews needed to understand that God used government, even that of King David, as a way of teaching them to anticipate his full and complete reign over the world. For, in human history the kingdom of God would not be a place over which Yahweh exerts physical power. Rather it will be made up of those who love Yahweh by the power and presence of the Holy Spirit. Laws that are imposed control populations. Love for Yahweh, however, works an obedience out from the inside. This was always God's design for humanity during the eons between the fall and Christ's final return. The Holy Spirit has been conquering the hearts of his people as he builds a mighty kingdom of countless people who love Yahweh above all other things.

JEREMIAH 23:1-8, 31:31-34

"Woe to the shepherds who destroy and scatter the sheep of my pasture!" declares the Lord. Therefore, thus says the Lord, the God of Israel, concerning the shepherds who care for my people: "You have scattered my flock and have driven them away, and you have not attended to them. Behold, I will attend to you for your evil deeds, declares the Lord. Then I will gather the remnant of my flock out of all the countries where I have driven them, and I will bring them back to their fold, and they shall be fruitful and multiply. I will set shepherds over them who will care for them, and they shall fear no more, nor be dismayed, neither shall any be missing, declares the Lord.

"Behold, the days are coming, declares the Lord, when I will raise up for David a righteous Branch, and he shall reign as king and deal wisely, and shall execute justice and righteousness in the land. In his days Judah will be saved, and Israel will dwell securely. And this is the name by which he will be called: 'The Lord is our righteousness.'

"Therefore, behold, the days are coming, declares the Lord, when they shall no longer say, 'As the Lord lives who brought up the people of Israel out of the land of Egypt,' but 'As the Lord lives who brought up and led the offspring of the house of Israel out of the north country and out of all the countries where he had driven them.' Then they shall dwell in their own land." . . .

"Behold, the days are coming, declares the Lord, when I will make a new covenant with the house of Israel and the house of Judah, not like the covenant that I made with their fathers on the day when I took them by the hand to bring them out of the land of Egypt, my covenant that they broke, though I was their husband, declares the Lord. For this is the covenant that I will make with the house of Israel after those days, declares the Lord: I will put my law within them, and I will write it on their hearts. And I will be their God, and they shall be my people. And no longer shall each one teach his neighbor and each his brother, saying, 'Know the Lord,' for they shall all know me, from the least of them to the greatest, declares the Lord. For I will forgive their iniquity, and I will remember their sin no more."

The Promise for God's People

The Jews took Palestine back from the Seleucid empire in the third century BC and, for the second time in their history, established a political kingdom under their own reign. The capital of the Hasmonean kingdom was the temple government called the Sanhedrin. The Sanhedrin instituted and enforced laws to secure Israel's political identity. By the normal means of mankind, the Jews joined the wide road of the world's ways. But their success was short lived.

Roman soldiers entered Palestine in 63 BC and then occupied the land thirty years later. When Jesus was born, the Jews were losing all hope of restoring their political independence. Rome was far more powerful than the Seleucids; the Jews were far less unified than they had been under the Hasmonean kings. They knew they would need a powerful leader, so they looked back at the prophetic books which spoke of a coming king.

Jesus claimed to be the object of the prophets, which set the Jewish leaders on edge. He did not pick up a normal sword or rally the people into a political unit. Rather he claimed to restore his people's hearts, not their power. He bound up the weakest and the poorest. But worst of all he attacked the Jewish political leaders. Jesus became an enemy to the Jews' political ambitions, and so they missed the glorious truth of his teachings: it is by grace that Yahweh will redeem Israel and then the whole world back to a loving relationship with him. From Genesis 3 on, Yahweh has been anticipating the grand wedding feast, where he and his people will be joined in love for eternity.

DECEMBER 22

The Point of the Story

In Genesis 3, God not only spoke a promise about his plan to redeem the world, but also delivered a prophecy about how the history of the world would unfold in the time before his final redemption. The world would be populated by two peoples, or what Moses described as two seeds. The serpent would be the parent of one group of people, which would issue from him the way that seeds grow on a plant. These seeds would share the same nature with their father plant. As the serpent twisted Yahweh's words to take power for himself, so his seed would distort God's laws in order to rule the world on their terms.

The other seed would come from Eve, who was created in the image of Yahweh. Her children would follow the pattern of the woman, whom God created so that she would live in intimate relationship with him. While God used the physical metaphor of seeds, the prophecy he delivered described the spiritual character of the two types of people who would inhabit and fill the earth: those who hate Yahweh and those who love him.

The history of the world is most often told according to political, cultural, and social narratives. Some nations gain military ascendency through a technological edge or a cultural innovation.

Egyptians created a centralized political and religious culture around the Nile as they enjoyed buffer zones of desert and wilderness. Persians developed a clear Manichaean religion which placed them on the side of cosmic good against cosmic evil and empowered them with an efficient administrative state. By this analysis, Israel had been a petty kingdom with a strong religious culture that allowed it to defeat its more decentralized neighbors. But this way of looking at history distracts from the real story of humanity: Israel was to lead those who feared the Lord in a world of those who follow in Satan's footsteps.

While the story of the seed of the serpent and the seed of the woman is the actual history of the world, it appears minor when compared to global affairs. Like the Ancient Hebrews, Christians often look to God to settle political scores with their enemies. The prophets seemed to see a day when God's people would conquer his foes as they followed his mighty King into battle. Hebrews understood this marvelous event as a moment when God would destroy Gentile nations. It seems that God's people easily ignore the true narrative of human history in favor of a worldly understanding. Yahweh will not defeat certain nations or peoples, rather he will destroy the seed of the serpent. Hebrews all too easily believed that, since they were part of Israel, they would be on the winning side. Through the mouths of the prophets, God mercifully retold the story of human history: the true victors will not be certain tribe of people but rather a certain kind of people—those redeemed by God.

The establishment of Yahweh's kingdom, therefore, will be a judgment against Satan's seed and a balm that would heal the suffering caused by the serpent's lies. Throughout the prophetic books, God referred to the day of victory and judgment as the great and awesome day of the Lord. In terms of military might, the Day of the

Lord would be unparalleled in all human history. Whereas human nations bring the might of armies to win battles, Yahweh would bring the might of angels. Whereas human governments exert natural powers, Yahweh would use supernatural powers. But these elements of the Day of the Lord pale in comparison to what Yahweh would accomplish through his mighty power. Yahweh planned to bring his awesome power to bear on Satan to make all things new, rid the world of evil, and establish an eternal reign of peace.

In the Day of the Lord, Yahweh will reestablish his reign over all the world as he crushes the sin that has so thoroughly marred his beautiful creation. His law will become the normal way of life; peace and love will define all human relationships. There is no alternative to this consummation of all of history. No nation, political movement, government, or economic system can realize all the hopes of humanity through the ages. What humans, because of their sin, are powerless to accomplish, God will do. He will remake the world as it ought to be. And the sign that this mighty kingdom had come would be the emergence of Elijah, the prophet to God's people in exile. For he will come once more to a people, cloaked in darkness, to point to the dawning of God's kingdom, the restoration of all things, and the destruction of the serpent's seed.

MALACHI 4

For behold, the day is coming, burning like an oven, when all the arrogant and all evildoers will be stubble. The day that is coming shall set them ablaze, says the Lord of hosts, so that it will leave them neither root nor branch. But for you who fear my name, the sun of righteousness shall rise with healing in its wings. You shall go out leaping like calves from the stall. And you shall tread down the wicked, for they will be ashes under the soles of your feet, on the day when I act, says the Lord of hosts.

"Remember the law of my servant Moses, the statutes and rules that I commanded him at Horeb for all Israel.

"Behold, I will send you Elijah the prophet before the great and awesome day of the Lord comes. And he will turn the hearts of fathers to their children and the hearts of children to their fathers, lest I come and strike the land with a decree of utter destruction."

The Promise Fulfilled

According to all the wisdom of the world, the Jews in first century Palestine were helplessly trapped. They had no military strength to exert. The Romans conquered the Jewish state without a war or even a battle, then used brute force to pacify them. The Jewish people were right to want independence from such a cruel and abusive power, but their frustrations and suffering lured them away from their true purpose. What many Jewish leaders failed to see was that, in their effort to win political freedom from their oppressors, they had become as spiritually dead as their oppressors. They turned God's laws into a means of social control and God's promises into the proof of their own cultural superiority.

The Jews, it seems, forgot that God's laws and promises were for the redemption of the world, Romans and Gentiles included. Jesus was clear: those who hate their enemies are those who belong to the serpent's seed. Rather than confirm the Jews' worldly ambitions, Jesus called his people to take up their crosses, die to the ways of this world, and follow him through the grave, into resurrection. Waiting for a worldly victory against their political enemies, the Jews failed to recognize that the kingdom had in fact come in the person of almighty Jesus. He conquered the serpent by taking upon himself the sins of his people. He gave his people exactly what they needed forgiveness and the power of the Holy Spirit to remain loyal to him above all other claims to power and all other promises of peace.

DECEMBER 23

The King Comes

All people know that they need salvation, even if the salvation for which they hope is that of a meal when they are hungry. Human beings are vulnerable creatures who need sustenance and protection in order to survive. We fear deprivation, which ultimately leads to our greatest fear—death. The solution we seek is salvation.

The world knows to look for salvation from the powerful. Men of strong families who possess physical might have in their hands the ability necessary to save people. In the ancient period, the strength of a person was indicated largely by his or her birth. The firstborn son of a family became the family's leader. In addition, tribes with the longest lineage and noblest heritage were naturally considered the most capable. National strength was squarely founded on the strength and loyalty of family members.

This principle was best exemplified in the dynasties that served as political backbones for most ancient societies. Each king rested on his relationship to a great ancestor who established the family line. The authoritative power of family lines and male birth was not the recourse of an ignorant people. In a time when military strength relied on pure manpower, the loyalty of kin and the backs of men determined the fate of nations. People considered that the gods determined birth order and ancestry, but the influence of a god only confirmed what was then common sense.

Yahweh shattered the world's political expectations. He claimed to be the king without heritage, the king who did not need the strength of men. He owned the cattle on a thousand hills, despite the human beings who claimed to possess them. Yahweh's power did not rest on any heritage or lineage; Yahweh's reign was not contingent on human strength. His royal position and almighty power came from his nature alone.

Not only did Yahweh reign in a way that seemed foreign to pagans of the ancient world, but it also appeared strange to his own people. He cared for his people in ways that seemed counterintuitive by ancient, as well as modern, standards. The world perceives the ability to rule as contingent upon power, fame, and heritage. God asserted his right to rule by caring for the poor and protecting bruised reeds. Yahweh does not need powerful men to protect his rule. Rather, Yahweh called his people to love him first, then to pursue justice for the weak. While the reign of all other kings is confirmed by the strength of family and the subservience of the outsider and the foreigner, Yahweh confirms his power by calling his family to become servants to the outsider.

In keeping with worldly views of power, cultures tell stories of great heroes who serve as examples for the people. But the people whom the Scripture set forward as examples were the lowest, not the greatest. God called leaders like David, the youngest and least-respected son of Jesse. He exalted Joseph, Jacob's youngest and least-respected son, who suffered rejection and even imprisonment.

It may be that the greatest hero of the Bible is Job, who refused to be disloyal to Yahweh even though Satan reduced Job to a child-less, disease-ridden heap of a person. With Yahweh's permission, Satan stole Job's strength, his wealth, and, most cruelly of all, his own children. Job's sons had made him important as they promised to continue his family line forward. Despite losing everything and becoming the most pitiable of all people in his day, Job did not turn from God. Job is the Bible's hero, the model citizen of Yahweh's kingdom, despite his human flaws. The Bible reverses every worldly expectation by reimagining power as weakness and justice as mercy. For God, the virgin of no social influence or power, from a poor family, served as the lineage of his great King.

Mary was the virgin fiancée to a poor member of the tribe of Judah. While the pattern of God's plan to save his people is consistent in the selection of Mary, his work was once again a surprise. By the every measure, she was the bottom of society. Yet her womb became the very seat of the universe's king. The birth of the king through Joseph's poor, virgin fiancée reconfigured the hope of God's people. Their king would not come with the trappings of worldly kings. With all their armies, chariots, and men, these kings are petty. They seek the world's acclaim as they follow its rules for power. In the unlikely birth of Jesus, Yahweh remade creation according to its original design—a world under the reign of the good King.

Christ's birth turned history back on itself. All human history had moved the world back to the disorder of Genesis 1:1. Jesus, however, began bringing the ruined world once again under his good reign. Sin ruined human relationships, which then devolved into injustice. Yahweh's king would establish justice between people. He would restore love between his people, who would then abhor the injustices of broken societies. The fall unleashed disease

and evil that worked all life towards death. Jesus would turn the
disorder of illness into the order of health, and the disunion of
death into eternal life. Jesus' reign would not be evident by the
standards of normal human expectations, rather it would. His reign
would in fact issue from the life of one who had no influence or
power in society.

He exalted the virgin's womb.

LUKE 1:26–55

In the sixth month the angel Gabriel was sent from God to a
city of Galilee named Nazareth, to a virgin betrothed to a man
whose name was Joseph, of the house of David. And the virgin's
name was Mary. And he came to her and said, "Greetings, O
favored one, the Lord is with you!" But she was greatly trou-
bled at the saying and tried to discern what sort of greeting this
might be. And the angel said to her, "Do not be afraid, Mary, for
you have found favor with God. And behold, you will conceive
in your womb and bear a son, and you shall call his name Jesus.
He will be great and will be called the Son of the Most High. And
the Lord God will give to him the throne of his father David, and
he will reign over the house of Jacob forever, and of his kingdom
there will be no end."

And Mary said to the angel, "How will this be, since I am a
virgin?"

And the angel answered her, "The Holy Spirit will come
upon you, and the power of the Most High will overshadow you;
therefore the child to be born will be called holy—the Son of
God. And behold, your relative Elizabeth in her old age has also
conceived a son, and this is the sixth month with her who was
called barren. For nothing will be impossible with God." And

Mary said, "Behold, I am the servant of the Lord; let it be to me according to your word." And the angel departed from her.

In those days Mary arose and went with haste into the hill country, to a town in Judah, and she entered the house of Zechariah and greeted Elizabeth. And when Elizabeth heard the greeting of Mary, the baby leaped in her womb. And Elizabeth was filled with the Holy Spirit, and she exclaimed with a loud cry, "Blessed are you among women, and blessed is the fruit of your womb! And why is this granted to me that the mother of my Lord should come to me? For behold, when the sound of your greeting came to my ears, the baby in my womb leaped for joy. And blessed is she who believed that there would be a fulfillment of what was spoken to her from the Lord."

And Mary said,

"My soul magnifies the Lord, and my spirit rejoices in God my Savior, for he has looked on the humble estate of his servant. For behold, from now on all generations will call me blessed; for he who is mighty has done great things for me, and holy is his name.

And his mercy is for those who fear him from generation to generation. He has shown strength with his arm; he has scattered the proud in the thoughts of their hearts; he has brought down the mighty from their thrones and exalted those of humble estate; he has filled the hungry with good things, and the rich he has sent away empty. He has helped his servant Israel, in remembrance of his mercy, as he spoke to our fathers, to Abraham and to his offspring forever."

And Mary remained with her about three months and returned to her home.

The Son of David

In choosing to come to his people through the humble station of a poor couple, who belonged to the poorest tribe of Israel and lived in one of the meanest of Israel's small towns, Yahweh bankrupted the world's expectations. But he also thwarted his own people's expectations as well. Some families of Israel had remained loyal to the temple despite Roman oppression. Their proud heritage of loyalty to the Jewish way of life granted them great social influence in Palestine. Yahweh could have chosen to bring his king through any number of strong and noble families. It stands to reason that so many leading families of the Sanhedrin rejected Jesus on the grounds of his lineage.

Jesus' lineage was more than a strange coincidence. Jesus preached mercy to sinners, touched lepers, and spoke to prostitutes. At the same time, Jesus castigated Israel's influential leaders, who wanted a king like every other nation—a man of strength with a powerful lineage. Jesus, however, humbled himself to the social reputation of being Mary and Joseph's son. He loved the poor and died a criminal's death. Jesus upended the world's false claims to power when he rose from the dead and confirmed that his kingdom of love, mercy, and justice stands over and against every human claim to power.

DECEMBER 24

God with Us

It is a wondrous thing that the king of all the universe was born at a time and place determined by a human emperor who ruled one of the world's most ruthless empires. Mary and Joseph were not able to choose the place of Jesus' arrival. Instead, they were forced to travel to the poor, out-of-the-way town in northern Palestine known as Bethlehem. Worse still was the fact that the town was so crowded with people, who had traveled to Bethlehem to participate in the census, that Mary was forced out of normal society and into a barn. While the uncomfortable surroundings are an important part of Mary's story, the fact that Jesus was born in exile from normal society carries tremendous weight. No one could claim that Jesus' influence came from his family, his place of birth, or the home into which he was born. By the standards that have governed the world since the fall of Adam and Eve, Jesus had nothing that would allow him to be counted as a leader or even as important.

To add insult to injury, Jesus' birth was not announced to Israel as an important event. Certainly, the historical accidents that led to Mary giving birth in a stable in the tiny town of Bethlehem could be written off as cruel fate. But when Yahweh confirmed Jesus' birth, he seemed to double down on his son's ignominy. It was common practice in that day to alert the citizens of a country when someone of noble lineage was born. Families would send messengers to the people of social stature so that the firstborn son would receive the blessing of important people. The announcement of the son's birth would begin his rise in society. Rather than send messengers to the

noble Jewish families of Palestine, Yahweh sent messengers to local
shepherds. Mary could be forgiven the fact that she was forced
to give birth in a stall, but she would never escape the humility of
entertaining shepherds.

In the first century Mediterranean world, shepherds were
considered the lowest members of society. They lived outside the
corridors of influence. They had no land holdings which they could
hand down from generation to generation. They were poor and
developed crude manners. They were routinely despised as outsid-
ers in the villages and towns. To make matters worse, shepherds
were not usually considered trustworthy enough even to serve as
witnesses in litigation. By any measure, the presence of shepherds
was an affront to any person's birth no matter his social stature.

But Yahweh's angels did not accidentally announce Christ's
birth to a field which happened to contain shepherds. From
the very beginning, Christ's position as king recast the world's
understanding of kingship. As Pilate would find out at the end of
Jesus' earthly ministry, Jesus was not just a king like other kings,
he was the King. While all other kings gain their authority and
station from the rules, patterns, and lineages of this world, Jesus
was king by his own divinity. He did not need the blessing of either
the Jews or the Romans; he did not even recognize their stations
in his kingdom. Christ was the king promised in Genesis 3 who
would overturn the sin of this world. He did not set out to reform
the world's political, social, cultural, and moral ways—he came to
upend them.

From the birthplace of King Jesus, some people are conspic-
uously missing. No members of the Sanhedrin visited the birth
of Israel's true king. Herod Antipas, one of four kings who ruled
Palestine on behalf of the Romans, only took interest in the popular

legends. Roman rulers of arguably the world's greatest empire in history never even took the slightest notice of Christ's birth. All of these were important in the perspective of the world. They all sought the strategic use of power and violence to ensure peace. But here in the tiny, humble town of Bethlehem, ragged and lowly shepherds heard the truth. They would become the first followers of the king who would bring peace to all peoples. His reign would mark a people who would join his kingdom out of all the nations of the world. His kingdom would grow in, though, and around every other kingdom in the world; his kingdom would outlast and outlive all of them.

It could be that the shepherds who cowered beneath the angels that night understood what the powerful in this world never seem to understand—that what humanity needs is not power or the suppression of enemies but rather a savior. Even that title is confusing in the world's understanding. Hebrews understood the importance of heroes like Samson, Gideon, and Jonas Maccabeus. Herod had seen his father stand up to the Jewish tribes in order to subjugate Palestine. Romans even bowed to the military genius and might of Augustus. But the angels spoke of a savior. He would not ride ahead of his people but rather serve them, raise them, and save them from sin and death.

LUKE 2:1–20

In those days a decree went out from Caesar Augustus that all the world should be registered. This was the first registration when Quirinius was governor of Syria. And all went to be registered, each to his own town. And Joseph also went up from Galilee, from the town of Nazareth to Judea, to the city of David, which is called Bethlehem, because he was of the house and lineage of David, to be registered with Mary, his betrothed, who was with child. And while they were there, the time came for her to give birth. And she gave birth to her firstborn son and wrapped him in swaddling cloths and laid him in a manger, because there was no place for them in the inn.

And in the same region there were shepherds out in the field, keeping watch over their flock by night. And an angel of the Lord appeared to them, and the glory of the Lord shone around them, and they were filled with great fear. And the angel said to them, "Fear not, for behold, I bring you good news of great joy that will be for all the people. For unto you is born this day in the city of David a Savior, who is Christ the Lord. And this will be a sign for you: you will find a baby wrapped in swaddling cloths and lying in a manger." And suddenly there was with the angel a multitude of the heavenly host praising God and saying,

"Glory to God in the highest, and on earth peace among those with whom he is pleased!"

When the angels went away from them into heaven, the shepherds said to one another, "Let us go over to Bethlehem and see this thing that has happened, which the Lord has made known to us." And they went with haste and found Mary and Joseph, and the baby lying in a manger. And when they saw it, they made known the saying that had been told them concerning this child. And all who heard it wondered at what the shepherds told them. But Mary treasured up all these things, pondering them in her heart. And the shepherds returned, glorifying and praising God for all they had heard and seen, as it had been told them.

King Over All Creation

The glory of the day when Christ was born is lost on all people to one degree or another. We are all taught to weigh events by cultural standards. There is no human measure that can fully make sense of what happened that first Christmas morning. A woman of no repute gave birth to a boy in an animal's stall, who was then visited by the lowest of Palestinian society. The fall has blinded us to reality. Only in the light of the Scriptures and the work of the Holy Spirit can God's people begin to see the truth. Despite all human claims to pleasure, glory, and power, the world has lived in agonizing separation from its Creator. Humans have devised lies to explain their own purpose in this world; they have invented comforts to convince themselves that they belong in this fallen world.

On that morning, Yahweh showed the utter dishonesty of the human heart. Under the chorus of angel voices, the world finally came face to face with its true meaning. It is alienated from its maker and in critical need of restoration. So deep is human blindness and deafness that for people desperately trying to make the brokenness of this world normal, the truth still goes unnoticed. Jesus is the longing of every human heart and the hope of every human ambition. In him the fullness of the Godhead dwelled among men to restore his people and, through them, to restore all the cosmos back to himself.

DECEMBER 25

The Word Became Flesh

In his introduction, John's Gospel diverges from the other three Gospels written by Matthew, Mark, and Luke. The other Gospels show that Jesus was the fulfillment of the Old Testament promises and stories. John confirms this, but he goes further. In the first three words, John draws us deep into the meaning of Christ as the fulfillment of not only every Jewish hope but, ultimately, every human hope. With the words, "In the beginning," John claims that every promise that looked forward to the Messiah first pointed back. For all that God promises in the Scriptures can be summarized as his plan to restore all that was lost. By his word, God created a good and beautiful universe. God's word is life itself, for it alone brings meaningful order out of chaos. From Genesis 3 to Malachi 4, all of God's prophets, priests, and kings have longed for his kingship to be restored to Genesis 1 and 2. For under King Yahweh alone will peace reign and beauty prevail in the universe.

John very carefully and intentionally chooses the word *logos,* not only because it captures God's creation power—the word that he spoke—but also because it harnesses five centuries of Greek and Hebrew thought. The Greeks had come to believe that this world is too confusing and temporary to create its own meaning. Only something transcendent, perfect, unchangeable, and eternal can give this fleeting life any meaning. One can study biology and learn how things live, but living things themselves cannot tell you why they live. It was Heraclitus who argued that the perfect and unchangeable truth which makes sense of the entire universe and gives it meaning is mind, or logos. The logos is the "logic" of all things. It is the truth upon which all truths rest. John's claim that the "logos" was in the beginning is a clear claim that God's word is the Truth of all reality, the Truth that makes sense of all truths.

But John is also a Jew and understands that the logos is more. Through the Old Testament, God provided metaphors and pictures for the one who would stand between this broken world and the holy God. Moses, Aaron, and Samuel are just three who mediated between the holy unchanging God and sinful humanity. John invokes not only the broad range of Greek philosophy in John 1:1, but also the fulfillment of Jewish theology. "In the beginning was the logos, and the logos was with God." But John then goes further: "He was God." In these three words John throws both Greek thought and Jewish theology over—the logos is a person, a "he." Jewish theology did not allow for a person to speak Yahweh's name, let alone see Yahweh. Here a person is *with* God and *is* God. The Greeks believed that the transcendent absolute was too perfect even to understand, yet for John the logos is a person.

In verse three John confirms the radical nature of this logos. This Word was the Creator of all things. This not a mere statement of physical creation—the power and wisdom to make things out of nothing. He is saying that the Word is the only source of all truth, goodness, and beauty. Not only was nothing made without him, but the Word is life itself. Life, the necessary condition for joy and pleasure, is in the Word and nowhere else. But the word "life" is not sufficient to explain who this logos is. He is also the light of men. He is the star around which all people must orient themselves to realize any goodness in their lives or in their world. He is the light that shines on all other truths. He is not a truth, but the one who makes all truths true. Jesus is the fulfillment of all the Jewish prophecies because he is the one who made the universe good.

John ends this Christmas poem with a claim that must reorient the way we see all of reality. Jesus is not *a* light but *the* light. All other forces—gods, idols, powers, ideas, institutions, and people—are derivative. John uses a very simple metaphor: light cannot be overcome by darkness. All other claims to order and goodness are darkness, and are therefore powerless competitors. For all of Rome's perceived power, it is nothing but the absence of light. No matter how persuasive any human king, society, idea, or scheme may be, it is as flimsy as a shadow. The deepest dark is powerless to influence let alone snuff out even the weakest light. In these verses we meet Christ—born in flesh, the logic of the universe, the meaning of our very existence, and the light against which no rival can stand.

JOHN 1:1–5

In the beginning was the Word, and the Word was with God, and the Word was God. He was in the beginning with God. All things were made through him, and without him was not any thing made that was made. In him was life, and the life was the light of men. The light shines in the darkness, and the darkness has not overcome it.

Merry Christmas!

The Now and
THE NOT YET

The Apostle John was not a mere theorist who was taken with the idea of Jesus. Upon meeting this wandering teacher, John left the promise of a steady living and a good reputation to follow the one most called a radical. The experience changed everything for him. He would devote his life to teaching about Christ's kingship and the salvation people could find in his name. It may be that John captured in first words of his Gospel his own transformation, from a citizen of earth to a citizen of the kingdom of heaven. In case his readers missed his main point for writing down what he experienced, John claimed that he did what he did, "so that you may believe that Jesus is the Christ, the Son of God, and that by believing you may have life in his name." (John 20:31b) From his experiences with Jesus, John eventually wrote the words that would spell out the hope of every Christian: King Jesus is "the Alpha and the Omega, the first and the last, the beginning and the end" (Revelation 22:13) "would make "all things new." (Revelation 21:5a)

John did not write his words in vacuum, but to a people who had despaired of all hope. In two devastating invasions, God brought his judgment down on Israel. In 722 BC the Assyrians sacked and destroyed the northern kingdom, then dragged its citizens back to Assyria. In 586 BC God raised up a second superpower, the Babylonians, to destroy the southern kingdom, Judah. Together these two events were a second fall from the garden. As Yahweh brought his people out of Egypt, he pointed them towards a new land that would flow with milk and honey. The garden joys of the promised land would be the byproducts of a land over which Yahweh himself ruled. Like humanity's first home, this second home would be a place under God's perfect reign. And, like God's relationship with Adam and Eve, he gave the Hebrews an ultimatum—obey his law and live in prosperity and peace or seek another king and suffer exile. Exile from Israel, Jerusalem, and the Temple confirmed that the Hebrews relationship with their God was broken.

Yet, at the very moment when God was stirring the Assyrians to hasten Israel's judgment, he spoke through the prophet Isaiah about a new time when the exile, not yet happening, would be over. For modern people, such as we are, the fall of Israel and the return of the Jews, in the fourth century BC, are just small subplots hidden behind major historical events like the triumph of the Athenians or the rise of the Roman empire. However, according to the Scriptures, these mighty powers, along with Assyrians, Babylonians, Chinese, Americans, or Europeans, are the subplots. All of history hinges on the relationship between God and his people. Isaiah's prophecies about the son of David, the shoot of the stump of Jesse, ascending his throne speak of the actual hinge of all human history. His birth would bring one era to end and begin a new era.

While the world, in exile from its Creator, slept through the birth of its king, the celebration of the angels burst out of their heavenly home and over poor shepherds. Prophets like Simeon and Anna called to those in Jerusalem, saying that humanity's exile was over. But greater than all of these was Elijah, who returned to Israel to call it away from spiritual exile, from the worship of idols, and back to fealty to Yahweh. John the Baptist became the new center of Jewish religion. His message was clear: the end of time had come; the kingdom of Yahweh was at hand. Yahweh himself confirmed John's message when he brought Jesus out to the Jordan River and then, while the waters of baptism poured over his son, proclaimed from his eternal throne, "This is my son!" The eternal king had come; the kingdom was now at hand.

Then his loving Father called Jesus out to meet with the serpent himself. Jesus not only started a new age of the world, but he also relived Adam and Eve's temptation. Instead of facing the serpent's temptation among a land of plenty, however, Jesus faced the tempter in a wilderness and himself on the brink of starvation. Yet the second Adam succeeded in every way that Adam and Eve failed. For Adam and Eve sacrificed their relationship with Yahweh to gain the world, but Jesus surrendered his life in perfect obedience to his loving father.

During his ministry, Jesus showed what was to come. He reversed the consequences of sin—disease, hunger, and death. He created food from nothing. He restored sight and made the crippled walk. Jesus reversed incurable diseases, such as leprosy, and he raised the dead. Although few understood it at the time, Jesus' miracles did not represent the final realization of his kingship; they were acts of love which inaugurated his reign. These miracles pointed to a time when the king would assume his throne, rule over the universe, and bring a New Jerusalem from heaven to earth. But before he ascended to his rightful throne (according to God's promise of Genesis 3), Jesus needed to engage in one final task, a battle of cosmic proportions.

The seed of the woman would have to suffer a devastating strike on the heel. The curse which Adam and Eve brought to all of humanity would fall on the Messiah with all its malignant force. Jesus not only died physically but suffered the ignominious death of a Roman crucifixion. Roman guards, who obeyed a petty, earthly tyrant, treated the universe's rightful king like a common criminal. But the second half of God's great promise changed everything. In the very strike that humiliated the Christ, God redeemed every sin his people had committed. Two days later, Jesus delivered Satan the final blow. In a crack of thunder and lightning, the Messiah crushed Satan's skull. Death—the law of Satan's rule over a broken world—now lay in ruins. Jesus did not just cripple Satan, he destroyed Satan's power.

By striking Satan in the head, Jesus became the king of this world. Ever since the fall of Adam and Eve, death had reigned over this world. All the works of mankind found their end in the tomb. Death sapped the strength men needed to overturn the thorns and thistles of this world. Nothing humanity did could overcome the end towards which all people moved. But the resurrected Christ is now the king of this world. Human life does not end in the grave, for death has become a doorway, not an impenetrable barrier. Death now serves the king. He works his plans for his people through the tomb, not despite it. Disease and war now play their part under the sovereign reign of our king. Nothing rivals his powerful kingship.

Bursting from the grave, Christ confirmed his kingship and inaugurated a new world. Death is now temporary. Though once as impenetrable as the Red Sea, death is now an open door, a dry and safe pathway that will bring God's people into eternal relationship with their king. Jesus made this quite clear when he appeared to his disciples and proclaimed that all power had been given to him. Then he ascended into heaven and took his rightful place at the right hand of Yahweh. In the ascension Jesus did not leave the world—he entered it. He did not go away, but he came into his inheritance as the Prince of all Creation. The kingdom of our God and of his Christ is now. And yet, we live in a world still broken by sin and death. With John the Baptist we cry out, "Are you the one who is to come, or shall we look for another?" (Luke 7:20)

Christ inaugurated his eternal reign on that glorious resurrection morning, but he did not yet finalize his reign. While among his disciples, he spoke of sheep that were not yet in the flock; at his ascension, he commanded that his kingship be preached to all peoples of all nations. In his eternal wisdom, God has delayed the realization of his son's full and perfect kingship. Yet God has not left us alone to wait.

Jesus promised to be with his people, even to the end of this second age of humanity's history. From his throne, Jesus has sent out the Holy Spirit, who indwells his people and forms them into a new Israel. While the world carries on its own temporal and doomed agendas, the Holy Spirit is building an eternal kingdom through the unity of his followers, the preaching of the gospel, and the ministry of love. In his Church, the reign of Christ is now. The people of his Church obey his laws with hearts made alive by the Spirit, and in so doing they stand against all those who oppose the only true king.

Christians are those who now live for, and under, Christ. We form the Church, which is the embodiment of his reign on earth. Christ calls his people to leave the petty kings of our world and become citizens of his heavenly kingdom. And yet we live in a world still governed by other monarchs. Cultural leaders determine

who fits in and who does not. Governments still enforce their
visions of justice. Economic players and processes decide who
has plenty and who does not. While we learn to navigate these
powers, and negotiate with them to survive, we do not owe them
final loyalty. In all this we affirm that Christ is king now, and that
his kingdom will yet be. And we look forward to the consummation
of his reign when we join our king around the table which he will
richly supply out of his awesome goodness.

DECEMBER 26

He Tabernacled Among Us

In the first several verses of chapter 1, John's Gospel reveals
Christ's true character so that no one would misunderstand: "And the
Word became flesh and dwelt among us, and we have seen his glory,
glory as of the only Son from the Father, full of grace and truth." (John
1:14) In Jesus, God returned to this world to fulfill every true desire
and hope that human beings have. According to the testimony of the
entire Old Testament, in knowing God we will finally understand
ourselves, others, and the world. This was impossible through the
temple, as it was also through the tabernacle or the tent of meeting.
Christ's birth in Bethlehem unwound the curse of humanity's sin, for
in Christ God himself had come into the world to dwell with us. In
Christ we now know Yahweh and, by knowing him, we can become
part of his work to restore all things under his kingship.

John is clear: this type of restoration cannot happen by the
religious, moral, or political practices of Israel. God's presence

first came to Israel when Moses delivered the law. But God did
not intend for the law to be the path by which he returned to his
people. The law, as Paul argues in Galatians, only points us to the
Christ (Galatians 3:24). Christ alone must bridge the gap between
God and man by grace, not law. The law (for Paul, not a moral law
but the entire religious life of Israel) could not bring sinful humanity back to its creator; by Christ's death and resurrection alone can
people enter once again into a loving relationship with their God.

JOHN 1:6-18

There was a man sent from God, whose name was John.
He came as a witness, to bear witness about the light, that all
might believe through him. He was not the light but came to
bear witness about the light.

The true light, which gives light to everyone, was coming
into the world. He was in the world, and the world was made
through him, yet the world did not know him. He came to his
own, and his own people did not receive him. But to all who
did receive him, who believed in his name, the gave the right to
become children of God, who were born, not of blood nor of the
will of the flesh nor of the will of man, but of God.

And the Word became flesh and dwelt among us, and we
have seen his glory, glory as of the only Son from the Father,
full of grace and truth. (John bore witness about him, and cried
out, "This was he of whom I said, 'He who comes after me ranks
before me, because he was before me.'") For from his fullness
we have all received, grace upon grace. For the law was given
through Moses; grace and truth came through Jesus Christ. No
one has ever seen God; the only God, who is at the Father's
side, he has made him known.

The Final Temple

The most terrible consequence of humanity's fall has been the ruin of our relationship with God. In the moments after Adam and Eve fell, they intuitively understood their new reality. The peace and glory of their lives was swallowed up with fear and guilt. They ran from each other and then from God to what cover the bramble could afford. This act was prophecy. They knew what now defines our lives: a sinful people cannot see a holy God. Adam and Eve hid from God, who would thereafter hide himself from mankind. As John states, "No one has ever seen God; the only God." (John 1:18)

But the holy God did not abandon the human race. From the moment humanity fell he put into motion a plan to reenter his world. He spoke to Abel, Noah, and Abraham. These personal relationships set the stage for a grander plan. He then rescued Israel from Egypt so that he could have a physical presence with all his people in the tent of meeting. Although God shielded his presence with ceremony and priestly work, nonetheless he was with his people. The tent then became a tabernacle which was more substantial and enduring.

But his greatest work of condescension (until Christ's birth) was the temple. Solomon's temple was a permanent home, fixed in Jerusalem. Even though priests alone could enter the holy of holies, Israel could still find God in a fixed place to seek him out and commune with him. So important was his presence with them, that they built their culture and their society around his presence.

This work of God was not only Israel's hope but the greatest hope of all mankind. For as God himself is the fulfillment of all human desires, so his presence in Israel represented the goal of all human efforts to realize joy, peace, and fulfillment. Not having the temple, humanity has busied itself making idols, gods, philosophies, and governments that have all been poor substitutes for God himself, the Word.

The revolution of Christmas is that in this child who was born under a star, God finally revealed to humanity his mind, heart, and beauty. John understood that human beings had made sincere efforts to find God. The word "light" in John 1 is the Greek word *phos*, which New Testament writers used both to mean "light" as well as "fire." Light makes people able to see, while fire is a prerequisite for civilization. It gives warmth, but it is also a catalyst that cures food and hardens wood. According to John, Jesus is the true light, the one for whom all humans have been searching. He is at once the final hope of all people and the foundation and condition of all those hopes.

Although Christ is the light and the fire of human life, the world chose to reject him. Worse than this, his own people, who had the Scriptures and the traditions, rejected him as well. The people who had built their entire world around the presence of God, turned their backs on him when he came.

It may be that the Jews did not have a clear understanding of what came after temple. In fact, most Jews considered the temple the final iteration of God's presence. Upon seeing Christ, the Jews should have immediately realized that their traditions of priesthood, feasts, sacrifices, and rituals were not the presence of God but rather blueprints for the true temple. The writer of Hebrews described all that God had provided for Israel since Moses as shadows of the real temple—Christ himself (Hebrews 8:1-5).

In John's imagery, the religious practices of Israel are similar to the activities of a blind person who must feel his way around the temple—ephods, garments, sheep, blood, holy furniture—in order to piece together a picture of what the temple really is. They could not see in their mind's eye that these were only shapes and patterns of God's true and lasting presence, Christ himself. At his appearing, all Jews should have finally understood that they performed all these wonderful ceremonies so that they would know the Christ when he came.

DECEMBER 27

Church of Jews and Gentiles

Through his life, death, and resurrection, Jesus—the true Israel—accomplished all that his people failed to accomplish, and he embodied all the promises God had given them. As the Hebrews lived and died over the generations from Abraham to John the Baptist, so they carried with them the very architecture of God's work of recreation. Born of Abraham's seed, Christ redeemed the Gentile through Israel's cultural life, not despite it. The history of the covenants, the law, the rituals of sacrifices, and the temple all came out of Israel's history. Rather than abandon those things, Jesus realized all of them in himself so that he might offer the entire promises of Israel to the rest of the world. In this way Jesus built upon the rubble of Israel's earthly kingdom an eternal kingdom in which both Jew and Gentile would love and serve Yahweh, the King of glory.

EPHESIANS 2:11-22

Therefore remember that at one time you Gentiles in the flesh, called "the uncircumcision" by what is called the circumcision, which is made in the flesh by hands—remember that you were at that time separated from Christ, alienated from the commonwealth of Israel and strangers to the covenants of promise, having no hope and without God in the world. But now in Christ Jesus you who once were far off have been brought near by the blood of Christ. For he himself is our peace, who has made us both one and has broken down tin his flesh the dividing wall of hostility by abolishing the law of commandments expressed in ordinances, that he might create in himself one new man in place of the two, so making peace, and might reconcile us both to God in one body through the cross, thereby killing the hostility. And he came and preached peace to you who were far off and peace to those who were near. For through him we both have access in cone Spirit to the Father. So then you are no longer strangers and aliens, but you are fellow citizens with the saints and members of the household of God, built on the foundation of the apostles and prophets, Christ Jesus himself being the cornerstone, kin whom the whole structure, being joined together, grows into la holy temple in the Lord. In him you also are being built together into a dwelling place for God by the Spirit.

The Church Universal

In Christ Jesus the kingdom has come. Through his ministry, Christ inaugurated God's final and permanent presence with his people. He made it clear that the evils of disease, blindness, and death were the physical consequences of humanity's catastrophic separation from Yahweh, and, by overcoming these disorders, he began the work of restoring this broken world. As God promised from the beginning, the seed of the woman restored the people's relationship with God when he crushed the seed of the serpent. After his resurrection, Jesus proclaimed that all power had been given to him over heaven and earth. He crushed death; he destroyed Satan's grip on the world, then he told his disciples that he saw Satan falling from the heavens like a falling star.

Amidst the bramble and thistles of this broken world, Jesus laid the foundations of a kingdom. This had always been God's promise. He called the Hebrews out of Egypt so that they might be a kingdom of priests. Their life together under his law and around his temple would begin the world all over again. Redemption according to God's plan was always going to be a physical reality, a society of people in history who rejected the serpent's lies and ordered their political, economic, cultural, and religious lives around God's word alone. This was the purpose for which he called Israel.

But Israel failed to remain loyal to Yahweh. They altered their cultural practices to imitate those of the surrounding nations. The men God called to be faithful to him took foreign wives, who drew their hearts into idolatry. Like Esau, Israel sold its birthright to satisfy earthly appetites. Like Eve, the Hebrews determined that the fruit of the Tree of the Knowledge of Good and Evil looked delicious enough to turn away from Yahweh's word. As Israel abandoned Yahweh, they also rejected their reason for existence.

Instead of heeding Christ's preaching and returning to God, the Jews looked back across their long history and determined that it was their national and familial heritage that made them special. Gentiles were the real danger to their national success. As with other nations, Israel came to believe that its god fought for its success, thereby confirming the importance of its people. The Jews came to believe that Yahweh loved them because they were special, and so they forgot that God called them to be a kingdom of priests. God did not love the Jews because they were special, rather the Jews were made special because God loved them.

Despite their sin and disloyalty, God had given the Jews the greatest gift that could be bestowed on any people. He gave them his law to teach them how to be his people. Yahweh gave Israel the temple which was his home on this earth. These realities were so important that they formed the historical framework for the final coming of God to his people, whose presence was the real reason for Israel's existence. These things would also serve as the context for God's return to his creation. Jesus was born according to the law of Moses, which Israel alone possessed. Jesus was committed to the temple because it was his Father's house. God created, saved, and maintained Israel, despite its great sins, so that it might become the physical, religious, and cultural space in which Jesus would inaugurate his work of redeeming the world back to himself.

While Israel formed the very place of God's work of recreation, the final goal of that work was always universal. At the very beginning of his redeeming work, Yahweh told Abraham that he would become a blessing to every nation. Israel imagined that it was God's only work of redemption, even though God had made it clear that it was only the beginning of that work. God planned to bring all the world back to himself through Israel's loyalty and obedience. Around his house, his temple, all the nations would gather to learn his peace and serve his glory.

DECEMBER 28

Salvator Mundi

Jesus is the bridge between fallen, broken humanity and the holy Yahweh. This mystery has always proven too difficult for human beings to understand, even though it is clear enough to help all people finally make sense of themselves and their world. Jesus is the same Word who, at the beginning of the universe, brought all things into creation, and he is the Word spoken to humanity for its redemption. Jesus brings the holy, perfect, and awesome God of all creation to sinful, broken, and suffering human beings. In his flesh and by the Spirit, he restores to Yahweh all that sin has taken and will make the cosmos what it was meant to be under his perfect reign.

COLOSSIANS 1:15-23

He is the image of the invisible God, the firstborn of all creation. For by him all things were created, in heaven and on earth, visible and invisible, whether thrones or dominions or rulers or authorities—all things were created through him and for him. And he is before all things, and in him all things hold together. And he is the head of the body, the church. He is the beginning, the firstborn from the dead, that in everything he might be preeminent. For in him all the fullness of God was pleased to dwell, and through him to reconcile to himself all things, whether on earth or in heaven, making peace by the blood of his cross.

And you, who once were alienated and hostile in mind, doing evil deeds, he has now reconciled in his body of flesh by his death, in order to present you holy and blameless and above reproach before him, if indeed you continue in the faith, stable and steadfast, not shifting from the hope of the gospel that you heard, which has been proclaimed in all creation under heaven, and of which I, Paul, became a minister.

The Fullness of the Godhead

Moses presented the Hebrews with a truth so strange that they never fully understood it: Yahweh is the source of all life who in himself makes all things real. The things of this world are only meaningful because he gives them meaning. He makes beauty beautiful, truth true, and goodness good. It was as difficult for the Hebrews as it is for us to understand that the value and meaning of what we see in this world is only borrowed. Health, wealth, and strength seem to be valuable in and of themselves.

The Hebrews felt in their bodies the evil of slavery and so saw freedom from Egypt as a good in and of itself. They believed that the purpose of having strength was to defend their families. But in the creation story, Moses reframed the Hebrew's universe. All the wonder of this world had a beginning in the mind of God and exists to serve his purposes alone. There is no source of meaning other than the word of Yahweh. In practical terms, freedom from

Egypt was only valuable because it allowed Israel to live out its true purpose—worship of Yahweh.

Over a thousand years after Moses, the Greeks concluded that they must have learned from Moses' teachings. The cultures of the Ancient Near East and the Mycenaeans of Ancient Greece lived in a world that was valuable on its own. The gods gave life, food, and victory as the only gifts worth having. But philosophers began to see what Moses had revealed. The good of this world is only borrowed from something more excellent. The wonders of this broken and changing world are only good for a brief moment and only for a few people.

If anything is to make humans truly happy, it must come from and point toward that which is absolutely good. Pleasure in this world is only valuable if it comes from an experience with something that is eternally, permanently, and absolutely beautiful. Truth, they discovered, cannot be found by looking at the constantly changing and eroding realities of this world. Truth must be ideas that agree with that which is unchanging and never erodes.

Paul understood both the Hebrew and Greek thought. Both cultures understood that the things of this world are not valuable in and of themselves, but are valuable only in service to that which is ultimate and transcendent. What both ancient pagans and modern secularists fail to realize is that this world cannot contain in itself the reason for life, nor the purpose for survival.

The ancient Hebrews and Greeks came to understand that knowing the transcendent and perfect is necessary for meaningful life—this was a cultural, religious, and philosophical revolution. However, neither of them could know finally what that absolute was. For the Hebrews, Yahweh was too holy to be seen, so perfect that his name could not be spoken. God made it clear that seeing him or even touching his presence meant instant death (death of Uzzah, II Samuel 6).

For the Greeks the absolute had to be changeless and pure such that it could not be found in a physical universe of change and corruption. While the human body itself was temporary and always corroding, it could not experience the perfect and transcendent. The Greeks believed that the mind alone, through philosophy, could grasp the absolute. Unfortunately, the Greeks found that no two minds could agree on what absolute reality was. Philosophy splintered into warring factions and descended into endless disagreements.

Paul saw that both the Hebrews and Greeks were right about the fact that absolute and perfect alone could makes sense of human life, but they had both rejected the only one who could bring them to the transcendent—Christ. He alone is both human and the unchanging, holy, and perfect being. He is the ladder Jacob saw that brought humanity to God and God to humanity

But the Greeks were scandalized by Paul's teachings. The Greeks knew that the transcendent, which made sense of the world, had to be impersonal in order to be incorruptible. For the transcendent God to take on human flesh, a flesh that bore the wounds of a humiliating execution, was irrational to the Greeks.

Likewise, the Jews could not imagine that the holy Yahweh, whose name was too holy to utter out loud, could weep for Lazarus or sit down to supper with tax collectors. How could the holy Yahweh touch a leper? To the Jews, Jesus had committed the worst of blasphemies by claiming to be the holy God. To the Greeks, Jesus had exhibited absolute irrationality by claiming to be the transcendent logos that alone gives purpose and meaning to all things.

Paul understood who Christ is. He is the truth that humanity has always needed. He is the transcendent, holy God who makes all reality meaningful; he is the Galilean Jew who tenderly embraces the sinner. He is the author of life who took death upon himself to save his people. He is the Word of God who brings order to the chaos of a world broken by sin. He is, in his flesh, the redeemer who brings the cosmos back to its Creator—the one who restores all things.

DECEMBER 29

True Reality

Jesus was the beginning of all things and will be the end of all things. He created the cosmos and thereby set the pattern for every one of its parts. His kingship will also be the complete and perfect end of the universe and humanity. But Jesus is more than just he who began all things and in whom all things will finally realize their perfect purpose. Jesus is also the summary of all things. Philosophies and religions in this world all try to connect the beginning of things to their end. The disjunction between these two things is unbridgeable in the human mind. We cannot trace this world back to a beginning that makes sense of what we see. What we see in this world does not appear to be moving towards a particular end that gives our world meaning. Christ is he who, in his person, connects our world to its origin and to its final destination.

HEBREWS 1

Long ago, at many times and in many ways, God spoke to our fathers by the prophets, but bin these last days he has spoken to us by his Son, whom he appointed the heir of all things, through whom also he created the world. He is the radiance of the glory of God and the exact imprint of his nature, and he upholds the universe by the word of his power. After making purification for sins, he sat down at the right hand of the Majesty on high, 4 having become as much superior to angels as the name he has inherited is more excellent than theirs.

For to which of the angels did God ever say,

"You are my Son,

today I have begotten you"?

Or again,

"I will be to him a father,

and he shall be to me a son"?

And again, when he brings the firstborn
into the world, he says,

"Let all God's angels worship him."

Of the angels he says,

"He makes his angels winds,

and his ministers a flame of fire."

But of the Son he says,

"Your throne, O God, is forever and ever,

the scepter of uprightness is the scepter of your kingdom.

You have loved righteousness and hated wickedness;

therefore God, your God, has anointed you

with the oil of gladness beyond your companions."

And,

"You, Lord, laid the foundation of the earth in the beginning, and the heavens are the work of your hands; they will perish, but you remain; they will all wear out like a garment, like a robe you will roll them up, like a garment they will be changed. But you are the same, and your years will have no end."

And to which of the angels has he ever said,

"Sit at my right hand until I make your enemies a footstool for your feet"?

Are they not all ministering spirits sent out to serve for the sake of those who are to inherit salvation?

Christ is the Logic of the Universe

God did not merely start history, abandon the universe, and then plan to take it back over at the end of history. He has ever been part of history, from laying the cloak of skin over Adam and Eve, to the Cold War, and beyond. Jesus has walked with all of humanity—from Adam's first breath until the great white throne judgment. Through Israel and then the Church, Christ is making possible the end for which he created all mankind. Thus, Christ is also the summary of all things, through whom God will realize his purpose of creation, his care over history, and the end toward which he is moving all things.

The world is not a random set of circumstances which humans harness for our own reasons. We tend to examine the fabric of history to detect some reason for our lives. We locate events and people in a picture which we hope will reveal to us the purpose for our existences, our communities, and our cosmos. We strain to explain wars, to appreciate nature, or to understand human suffering even though we know that such things are beyond us. All human experiences are just swishes of color in a grand painting that we do not get to see and that, therefore, makes no sense to us. From the perspective of mankind, history is an interesting but meaningless collection of brilliant colors and deep darkness.

Human history does not make sense to those who live through it. In fact, on its own terms, history is not capable of revealing its purpose, direction, or hope. Only the one who created all things and who will bring all things to their appointed end understands. Like an artist who must arrange and rearrange the paint colors to make a landscape appear on a canvas, so Yahweh reveals his masterpiece through the elements of history.

The difficulty for humanity is that until God restores all of creation, we are part of the painting process. The mixture of colors and lines cannot reveal to us what the master artist is doing through time. We make sense of some of the pieces: the need for physical and psychological health for human flourishing; the mathematical structure of the physical universe; the power of love and forgiveness in human relationships, etc. But the mural to which these small parts belong is beyond us.

What we do understand about human existence is a gift God has to granted us that we call "general revelation"—it shows us how to live well in this world. But he has given humanity so much more. By his grace, God also provided us with special revelation. While neither the paints, canvas, or brush strokes can clearly show us what he is doing from the beginning to the end (Ecclesiastes 3), he has spoken at times and places to his people. Through his Scriptures, God reveals his character as well as the essential components of redemptive plan. They reveal that while the major brush strokes and colors of the canvas in history may reflect mighty nations and powers, the smaller subjects of his work point to the purpose of the entire work. God granted to Israel, a small and embattled people in a dusty land, the place of prominence in his work of redemption.

God established familial systems of male inheritance along with complicated sacrificial systems in order to prepare the world for the way that he would redeem the cosmos back to himself. For over a thousand years, these measures accomplished no final end. They were merely flecks of shadow and light, each one amounting to nothing on its own. Even Israel grew weary of waiting for these brilliant flourishes to reveal the picture of which they were an essential part. Over time the Israelites transformed things like sacrifices, priestly offices, and national kings into the point of God's work rather than mere images of his final work.

For those Jews to whom God had given faith, however, the life of Israel was just a shadow of the promise to come. The patriarchs of Israel and the prophets who followed knew that God created Israel to anticipate the seed of the woman. When Jesus came, the various elements of the painting began to make sense. He is the meaning of the entire painting, from Abel's good sacrifices to the construction of Solomon's temple. For in Christ both the creation of the world and its redemption are joined together into the great and awesome work of Yahweh.

Both the Romans and the Jews of his day tried to make sense of Jesus by referring to their knowledge of history. They failed to realize that rather than use history to understand what God is doing, they needed to believe in what God was doing to understand history. The rise and fall of nations throughout time did not provide proper instruction for understanding the Messiah. Rather it was the character of the Messiah who finally made sense of the nations. While humanity has always sought to plug Christ back into God's grand painting of human history, it has failed to realize that he is the one about whom God has painted all of history. And by grace he assumes this place so that he might save his people from their sins and bring them to live with him for eternity.

DECEMBER 30

Abba

Christ, by his incarnation, traversed the infinite distance between Yahweh's holy character and his sinful people. Christ, by his crucifixion and resurrection, makes it possible for his sinful and broken people to live in relationship to the Holy God. Because of Christ we now call Yahweh "Abba," father. This truth is not merely a spiritual reality, although it is at least that. This work of Christ was also a historical act that began anew the recreation of the world. He bore in his flesh the curse of sin so that he might call out of this world a people through whom he would once again bring all the world under the sovereign power of his word. Through his Church by the work of the Holy Spirit, Jesus lays down stones and mortar, day by day, as he reconstructs the world as it was supposed to be before humanity rejected its Creator. Jesus is making the world new.

REVELATION 21

Then I saw a new heaven and a new earth, for the first heaven and the first earth had passed away, and the sea was no more. And I saw the holy city, new Jerusalem, coming down out of heaven from God, prepared as a bride adorned for her husband. And I heard a loud voice from the throne saying, "Behold, the dwelling place of God is with man. He will dwell with them, and they will be his people, and God himself will be with them as their God. He will wipe away every tear from their eyes, and death shall be no more, neither shall there be mourning, nor crying, nor pain anymore, for the former things have passed away."

And he who was seated on the throne said, "Behold, I am making all things new." Also, he said, "Write this down, for these words are trustworthy and true." And he said to me, "It is done! I am the Alpha and the Omega, the beginning and the end. To the thirsty I will give from the spring of the water of life without payment. The one who conquers will have this heritage, and I will be his God and he will be my son. But as for the cowardly, the faithless, the detestable, as for murderers, the sexually immoral, sorcerers, idolaters, and all liars, their portion will be in the lake that burns with fire and sulfur, which is the second death."

Then came one of the seven angels who had the seven bowls full of the seven last plagues and spoke to me, saying, "Come, I will show you the Bride, the wife of the Lamb." And he carried me away in the Spirit to a great, high mountain, and showed me the holy city Jerusalem coming down out of heaven from God, having the glory of God, its radiance like a most rare jewel, like a jasper, clear as crystal. It had a great, high wall, with twelve gates, and at the gates twelve angels, and on the gates the names of the twelve tribes of the sons of Israel were inscribed—on the east three gates, on the north three gates, on the south three gates, and on the west three gates. And the wall of the city had twelve foundations, and on them were the twelve names of the twelve apostles of the Lamb.

And the one who spoke with me had a measuring rod of gold to measure the city and its gates and walls. The city lies foursquare, its length the same as its width. And he measured the city with his rod, 12,000 stadia. Its length and width and height are equal. He also measured its wall, 144 cubits by human measurement, which is also an angel's measurement. The wall was built of jasper, while the city was pure gold, like clear glass. The foundations of the wall of the city were adorned with every kind of jewel. The first was jasper, the second sapphire, the third agate, the fourth emerald, the fifth onyx, the sixth carnelian, the seventh chrysolite, the eighth beryl, the ninth topaz, the tenth chrysoprase, the eleventh jacinth, the twelfth amethyst. And the twelve gates were twelve pearls, each of the gates made of a single pearl, and the street of the city was pure gold, like transparent glass.

And I saw no temple in the city, for its temple is the Lord God the Almighty and the Lamb. And the city has no need of sun or moon to shine on it, for the glory of God gives it light, and its lamp is the Lamb. By its light will the nations walk, and the kings of the earth will bring their glory into it, and its gates will never be shut by day—and there will be no night there. They will bring into it the glory and the honor of the nations. But nothing unclean will ever enter it, nor anyone who does what is detestable or false, but only those who are written in the Lamb's book of life.

The Purpose of History

The history of the universe is a story with a specific plot. It began with a garden of beauty and goodness. This garden, like any other of its kind, was a place of order and sustenance. Unlike other gardens, the organic splendor of Eden flowed out of the intimate relationship that Adam and Eve had with God and each other. Our first parents then imitated their Creator by ruling over Eden in obedience to his will. The garden was a glorious home, but it was also a promise of a better home yet to come.

The garden was incomplete; it was good, but not perfect. The word "perfect" means absolutely complete and lacking nothing. God did not make the world perfect in this sense. He created it and called it good, then called Adam and Eve to complete the work that he began. God placed his people over his world to tend it and expand it.

Just like the land around the garden, the entire globe was wondrous, but it was not yet as ordered as Eden. As God had brought order out of chaos, so he called Adam and Eve to imitate him by expanding the garden until they brought the entire globe under the order of God's word. God helped Adam in starting this work by naming all the animals. This was a kingly act of dominion, as naming the animals meant giving them definition and boundary. In cooperation with his creator, Adam began the work of extending God's perfect reign.

What would have happened in the world had Adam and Eve not fallen? In a world without sin, people without sin would have engaged in glorious, fulfilling, and effective work. All that Adam and Eve would have accomplished would have been clear reflections of God's creativity, direct revelations of his glory and holiness.

By God's promises, they would then have had children who would have followed Adam and Eve's example the same way that Adam and Eve followed God's. People in perfect relationship with each other and God would have brought holy order to the entire world. Human societies, animals, plants, weather, and human invention would have coexisted in perfect harmony as they extended from the Godhead.

Moses does not tell us how long Adam and Eve lived in the cycle of wondrous labor and glorious rest as they completed God's work of creation. Moses is clear, however, that the time of bringing God's order to the world ceased when Eve believed the serpent's word and Adam ate the fruit. Humans then took on the task of ordering the entire world through creative labor and having children. All their work, however, has been plagued with sin. For all its functional efficiency and beauty, human labor serves kings other than Yahweh. Ignoring the source of all goodness has poisoned human effort with disorder and death. And yet God did not abandon humanity to pure chaos. By his providence he has protected his image in mankind. Although replete with sin and evil, by God's grace, humans still bring life, improve survival, create beauty, and promote civic goodness.

History bears out a trend which proves to be a sickly shadow of what it ought to have been: Eden as the garden of God's presence was to grow with Adam and Eve's children. They would have increased in population until they needed towns and then cities. The image of God in mankind would blanket the earth with industry and community, with art and efficiency all toward one end—to be the place where God would dwell with his people in uninterrupted intimacy. While human sin has corrupted God's good plan, it is powerless to stop him from completing what he started. Neither

Adam nor Eve, nor all their progeny, could make God's good earth perfect, but Yahweh will complete what he began.

It is difficult to see how God will complete his work of creation if we simply view human history. The plot of nations and societies does not reveal the road to a perfect world. One thing that the Bible makes clear from the creation narrative to the last pages of Revelation is that only under the reign of Jesus Christ will the world be made perfect. He was the Word who brought the ordered garden of Eden out of the chaos of the world. He called Abraham to father a people who would become the agents of recreation. He died for his people's failures and was raised to sit at Yahweh's right hand so that he might finish what he started for the sake of his sinful people. All human hope now rests on what Jesus will do by his reign through the work of the Holy Spirit for the Father. He will bring the universe to completion as it was designed—Yahweh's permanent, eternal home among his people.

DECEMBER 31

The End is the Purpose

God has not abandoned his people to permanent exile from his healing love. Though his people have broken their relationship with the one true God by giving themselves to false gods, he has determined, by his own sovereign will, to bring them back to himself. On their own, they cannot restore what sin had taken, but Jesus loved his people so deeply that he took upon himself their diseases so that he might restore his people to Yahweh.

Christ gave himself for his people. He stood between them and God's wrath. He called them out of their relationships to the idols and gods of this world and restored them to the eternal love of their Father in heaven. He now waits to be reunited to his people in a wedding that was planned before the beginning of the world. God created human beings to join with him in an intimate relationship which Christ will realize. When Christ returns, Yahweh will preside over the wedding of Christ and his people, a union that will inaugurate an eternal kingdom of love and bring all the universe under his word.

REVELATION 22

Then the angel showed me the river of the water of life, bright as crystal, flowing from the throne of God and of the Lamb through the middle of the street of the city; also, on either side of the river, the tree of life with its twelve kinds of fruit, yielding its fruit each month. The leaves of the tree were for the healing of the nations. No longer will there be anything accursed, but the throne of God and of the Lamb will be in it, and his servants will worship him. They will see his face, and his name will be on their foreheads. And night will be no more. They will need no light of lamp or sun, for the Lord God will be their light, and they will reign forever and ever.

And he said to me, "These words are trustworthy and true. And the Lord, the God of the spirits of the prophets, has sent his angel to show his servants what must soon take place."

"And behold, I am coming soon. Blessed is the one who keeps the words of the prophecy of this book."

I, John, am the one who heard and saw these things. And when I heard and saw them, I fell down to worship at the feet of the angel who showed them to me, but he said to me, "You must not do that! I am a fellow servant with you and your brothers the prophets, and with those who keep the words of this book. Worship God."

And he said to me, "Do not seal up the words of the prophecy of this book, for the time is near. Let the evildoer still do evil, and the filthy still be filthy, and the righteous still do right, and the holy still be holy."

"Behold, I am coming soon, bringing my recompense with me, to repay each one for what he has done. I am the Alpha and the Omega, the first and the last, the beginning and the end."

Blessed are those who wash their robes, so that they may have the right to the tree of life and that they may enter the city by the gates. Outside are the dogs and sorcerers and the sexually immoral and murderers and idolaters, and everyone who loves and practices falsehood.

"I, Jesus, have sent my angel to testify to you about these things for the churches. I am the root and the descendant of

David, the bright morning star."

The Spirit and the Bride say, "Come." And let the one who hears say, "Come." And let the one who is thirsty come; let the one who desires take the water of life without price.

I warn everyone who hears the words of the prophecy of this book: if anyone adds to them, God will add to him the plagues described in this book, 19 and if anyone takes away from the words of the book of this prophecy, God will take away his share in the tree of life and in the holy city, which are described in this book.

He who testifies to these things says, "Surely I am coming soon." Amen. Come, Lord Jesus!

The grace of the Lord Jesus be with all. Amen.

Come, Lord Jesus

Death reaches backwards from our graves into the very fibers of our lives. We experience hunger, pain, and disease. But the curse of death is more devastating than the disorder it brings to our bodies. Death's influence in our lives can be measured by the innumerable plagues it unleashes on human relationships. Like a living organism that depends on the harmony between its parts and between itself and the world around it, so relationships are delicate. Love is a complicated organism that is built on trust, which only holds together only in states of extremely high order. Suspicion, fear, anxiety, distrust, anger, and a myriad of other pathogens disrupt the complex organic structures necessary to maintain life-giving relationships. In this world healthy relationships are under attack continually from outside and inside.

Disorder in relationships is normal to the human experience, but it is not how God designed them to work. God pulled Adam out of the dust for the purpose of living in a perfect relationship with him but in that, Adam was not to be alone. Adam then surveyed the entire creation for the purpose of finding a helper, one with whom he could enter into a life-giving intimacy. This was the purpose of Adam's existence, yet Adam could not find a suitable helper. And so, God created, out of Adam, a new person. Eve would not only make Adam complete and provide him with the gift of intimacy, it would also teach the both about the deepest reason for their own existence. Together they would find in their intimacy the dimensions and facets of their relationship with Yahweh.

Adam and Eve did not first taste death in their bodies when they sinned, but rather in their souls. The moment that they rejected God's governance over their lives, disease entered their relationship with each other. The complex order of trust disintegrated into tortured insecurity and vulnerability. They hid from God behind fig leaves from each other and behind Eden's lush vegetation. Like any disease, sin's true symptoms were only appreciated after it worked its disorder on the entire organism.

Adam and Eve's sin created the suspicion and fear that would ruin their family when it bore fruit in Cain's life. Trust broke down into control and tyranny. Love devolved into hate. The purpose for humanity now became its undoing. God made human beings to be in relationship with each other so that they might realize the depth and beauty of their relationship with God. Once they were separated from God, however, relationships became toxic.

While human beings weaponized relationships, God did not allow the purpose of humanity to die entirely. In his grace he allowed people to come together in intimate and life-giving bonds.

Despite the evil that plagues human experience, he continued to animate love between people. While human love is an unhealthy version of the true reality, it is still a picture of what God created humans to be. Men and women marry as a life-giving commitment in the face of sin's evil. Parents and children work without ceasing to forge healthy relationships that lead to flourishing against all the contagions of pride, greed, selfishness, and insecurity. Friends cling to one another despite the pains of slights and disagreements. In his goodness God upholds what sin means so thoroughly to destroy. But there is more to God's providence. He protects relationships in order to give human beings so many pictures, no matter how obscured by death, of our true reason for existence—to be in relationship with him.

Throughout Scripture, God draws on many metaphors to help his people understand who they are and why they exist. The most common is the picture of marriage, not because the Bible's authors canvased all other relationships to find a suitable analogy of God's relationship with his people, but because God created marriage to teach his people who he always meant for them to be. Against all human tendencies toward selfishness, a man and a women enter the marriage relationship to commit themselves to one another.

God designed marriage to teach very specific lessons about his relationship with his people. God cares for his people by giving them the garden, while his people reverence and love him. In this way the husband provides for his wife at his own expense, while the wife honors her husband at hers.

Under the Old Covenant, God called Israel into a redeeming marriage relationship with himself. He fought for her, rescued her, supplied her needs, and loved her; Israel was to give herself to him alone in worship and honor. God's love for Israel established the pattern for how he would redeem all the world back to himself. God will call his people out of all the broken relationships in this world to restore them to be joined with him in a loving and exclusive eternal marriage. In his eternal kingdom the relationship between Yahweh and his people will suffer no corruption; it will be freed from the diseases that plague all our relationships in this world. He will bring us out of our exile into a relationship with him that will know no disorder, brokenness, fear, shame, or alienation.

DANIEL R. SPANJER graduated from Nyack College with a BA in History and from Reformed Theological Seminary (Orlando) with a MA Theology. In April 2016, he successfully defended his dissertation at the University at Albany, SUNY. He has taught at Nyack College, University at Albany, and is currently the Chair of the Arts and Sciences Department and Professor of History at Lancaster Bible College. He also serves the college as the director of the Alcuin Society, a scholarly organization which serves campus faculty. Dan is a pilot and has worked as a mechanic, commercial fisherman, grant administrator and golf course greens keeper. He is married to Tara Spanjer, and they have three daughters: Meghan, Emily, and Katelyn.

Special thanks
to my pastor, Luke LeDuc,
for the feedback
(and title!) for this book.

MORE BOOKS *about*
the story of THE BIBLE

HOW TO SEE: READING GOD'S WORD WITH NEW EYES
Our understanding of biblical accounts often look nothing like
what actually is *in* the Bible. This book offers tools to love God
through a better approach to biblical interpretation.

GODLY CHARACTER(S): INSIGHTS FOR SPIRITUAL
PASSION FROM THE LIVES OF 8 WOMEN IN THE BIBLE
"... these 'great eight' propel you towards habits of godliness—
putting you in a place to receive grace and fall more deeply in
love with your savior ..."
—Robert William Alexander, author of *The Gospel-Centered Life at Work*

REVEALED: A STORYBOOK BIBLE FOR GROWN-UPS
"Revealed sets out to crush any notion that the Bible is a safe,
inspirational read. Instead the artwork here, historic and contem-
porary, takes a warts-and-all approach to even the most troubling
passages, trading well-meaning elision for unvarnished truth."
—J. Mark Bertrand—novelist and founder of the Bible Design Blog

NAILED IT: 365 READINGS FOR ANGRY
OR WORN-OUT PEOPLE
"... if you, like me, long for a devotional that is sharpening, witty,
and downright real, well then, you simply must read this book."
—Karen Swallow Prior, author of *On Reading Well: Finding the
Good Life Through Great Books*

SQUAREHALOBOOKS.*com*